First World War
and Army of Occupation
War Diary
France, Belgium and Germany

3 DIVISION
Divisional Troops
Royal Army Medical Corps
9 Field Ambulance
5 August 1914 - 31 July 1915

WO95/1407/3

The Naval & Military Press Ltd
www.nmarchive.com
Published in association with The National Archives

Published by

The Naval & Military Press Ltd

Unit 10 Ridgewood Industrial Park,

Uckfield, East Sussex,

TN22 5QE England

Tel: +44 (0) 1825 749494

www.naval-military-press.com

www.nmarchive.com

This diary has been reprinted in facsimile from the original. Any imperfections are inevitably reproduced and the quality may fall short of modern type and cartographic standards.

© Crown Copyright
Images reproduced by permission of The National Archives, London, England, 2015.

Contents

Document type	Place/Title	Date From	Date To
Heading	WO95/1407/2		
Heading	3rd Division Medical No.9 Field Ambulance Aug-Dec 1914		
Heading	War Diary of No.9 Field Ambulance III Division From 5th August 1914 To 31st August 1914		
War Diary	Southsea	05/08/1914	18/08/1914
War Diary	At Sea	19/08/1914	19/08/1914
War Diary	Rouen	20/08/1914	22/08/1914
War Diary	On March Valenciennes To St Waast	23/08/1914	23/08/1914
War Diary	At Bois La Crette	24/08/1914	25/08/1914
War Diary	Le Cateau	25/08/1914	26/08/1914
War Diary	On Night March To Estrees	26/08/1914	27/08/1914
War Diary	Outside Ham	27/08/1914	27/08/1914
War Diary	Varesnes	28/08/1914	28/08/1914
War Diary	Cutts-Vic-Sur-Aisne	29/08/1914	29/08/1914
War Diary	Le Chat Embarrasse	30/08/1914	30/08/1914
War Diary	Vauciennes	31/08/1914	31/08/1914
Miscellaneous	Expeditionary Force		
Miscellaneous	9th Field Ambulance	24/08/1914	24/08/1914
Miscellaneous	Detrainment And Billeting Order		
Miscellaneous	A Form Messages And Signals		
Miscellaneous	O.C. 9th Fd Amb	31/08/1914	31/08/1914
Miscellaneous	C Form (Original) Messages And Signals		
Heading	9th Fd Amb		
Miscellaneous	A Form Messages And Signals		
Miscellaneous	9th Fd Amb		
Miscellaneous	O.C. No.9 Field Ambulance		
Miscellaneous	O.C. 9th Field Ambulance	12/08/1914	12/08/1914
Heading	War Diary of No.9 Field Ambulance (C.Section)		
Miscellaneous	24 Aug Marked via Bavay-Hon		
Miscellaneous	Blaregnies Belgium	24/08/1914	24/08/1914
Heading	War Diary No9 Field Ambulance Volume II 121/1082 Sept 1914		
War Diary	Bouillancy	01/09/1914	01/09/1914
War Diary	Lesches	02/09/1914	02/09/1914
War Diary	La Logeartus	03/09/1914	03/09/1914
War Diary	On March	04/09/1914	04/09/1914
War Diary	Chatres	05/09/1914	05/09/1914
War Diary	Lumigny	06/09/1914	06/09/1914
War Diary	Le Martroy	07/09/1914	07/09/1914
War Diary	Orly	08/09/1914	08/09/1914
War Diary	Bezu	09/09/1914	09/09/1914
War Diary	Dammard	10/09/1914	10/09/1914
War Diary	Grand-Rozoy	11/09/1914	11/09/1914
War Diary	Braine	12/09/1914	30/09/1914
Miscellaneous	Headquarters 3rd Division	19/09/1914	19/09/1914
Miscellaneous	Headqrs 3rd Division O.C. 9 Field Ambulance	19/09/1914	19/09/1914
Miscellaneous	A Form Messages And Signals	17/09/1914	17/09/1914
Miscellaneous	O.C. 9th Fd Ambulance	14/09/1914	14/09/1914
Miscellaneous	O.C. No.9 Field Ambulance	15/09/1914	15/09/1914

Miscellaneous	O.C. 9th Fd Ambulance	16/09/1914	16/09/1914
Miscellaneous	Operation Order 9th Bde	11/09/1914	11/09/1914
Miscellaneous	O.C. No.9 Field Ambulance	09/09/1914	09/09/1914
Miscellaneous	A Form Messages And Signals	08/09/1914	08/09/1914
Miscellaneous	Order Of March		
Operation(al) Order(s)	Operation Order No.25 by Gen F.C. Shaw C.B. Coy Cmdg Right Column	06/09/1914	06/09/1914
Miscellaneous	A Form Messages And Signals		
Miscellaneous	No 9 Fd Ambce		
Miscellaneous	Messages And Signals		
Miscellaneous	A Form Messages And Signals		
Miscellaneous	O.C. 8th Field Ambulance	02/09/1914	02/09/1914
Miscellaneous	C Form (Original) Messages And Signals	01/09/1914	01/09/1914
Miscellaneous	A Form Messages And Signals		
War Diary	Vailly	22/09/1914	25/09/1914
War Diary	Courcelles	26/09/1914	30/09/1914
Heading	121/1967 Oct 1914 9th Field Ambulance Vol III		
War Diary	Braine	01/10/1914	01/10/1914
War Diary	Cramaille	02/10/1914	03/10/1914
War Diary	Troesnes	04/10/1914	04/10/1914
War Diary	Crepy	05/10/1914	05/10/1914
War Diary	Roberval	06/10/1914	06/10/1914
War Diary	Abbeville	07/10/1914	07/10/1914
War Diary	Port-Le-Grand	07/10/1914	08/10/1914
War Diary	Tollent	09/10/1914	09/10/1914
War Diary	Tangry	10/10/1914	10/10/1914
War Diary	L'Ecleme	11/10/1914	11/10/1914
War Diary	Cross Roads 1/2 Nr E of Lecornet Malo	12/10/1914	12/10/1914
War Diary	Zelobes	13/10/1914	15/10/1914
War Diary	Farm Houses 1/2 Mile N Of X Roads at C of Croix Barbee	16/10/1914	16/10/1914
War Diary	Rouge Croix	17/10/1914	22/10/1914
War Diary	Vieille Chapelle	23/10/1914	26/10/1914
War Diary	Zelobes	27/10/1914	30/10/1914
War Diary	About 1.m N Of Branoutre	31/10/1914	31/10/1914
Miscellaneous	O.C. 9th Field	01/10/1914	01/10/1914
Miscellaneous	3rd Division	02/10/1914	02/10/1914
Miscellaneous	A Form Messages And Signals	03/10/1914	03/10/1914
Operation(al) Order(s)	Operation Order No. 3 by Brig FC Shaw CB	04/10/1914	04/10/1914
Miscellaneous	Route		
Operation(al) Order(s)	Operation Order No 4 By Brig General Shaw CB Commdg Inf Bde	05/10/1914	05/10/1914
Miscellaneous	March Table		
Miscellaneous	Orders		
Miscellaneous	D.A.G. M.G for Orders for No 9 Field Ambulance		
Operation(al) Order(s)	Operation Order No.6 By Brig General F.C. Shaw CB Comdg 9th Infy Bde	08/10/1914	08/10/1914
Miscellaneous	March Table		
Operation(al) Order(s)	Operation Order No.7 By Brig Genl F.C. Shaw CB Commdg 9 Infy Bde	09/10/1914	09/10/1914
Miscellaneous	A Form Messages And Signals		
Miscellaneous	9 Fd Amb		
Miscellaneous	A Form Messages And Signals		
Miscellaneous	O.C. 9th Field Ambulance	12/10/1914	12/10/1914
Miscellaneous	A Form Messages And Signals		
Heading	121/2625 Nov 1914 No9 Field Ambulance Vol IV		

War Diary	La Clytte	01/11/1914	02/11/1914
War Diary	Bailleul-Nieppe Road	03/11/1914	03/11/1914
War Diary	Bailleul	04/11/1914	05/11/1914
War Diary	Ypres-Vlamertinghe	06/11/1914	06/11/1914
War Diary	Vlamertinghe	07/11/1914	19/11/1914
War Diary	Westoutre	20/11/1914	20/11/1914
War Diary	Berthen	21/11/1914	30/11/1914
Heading	121/3907 Dec 1914 No.9 Field Ambulance Vol V		
War Diary	Berthen	01/12/1914	13/12/1914
War Diary	Near Westoutre	14/12/1914	31/12/1914
Heading	3rd Division Medical 9th Field Ambulance 1915 Jan-1915 July		
Heading	8 Field Ambulance 1914 Aug To 1919 May 9 Field Ambulance 1914 Aug To 1915 July		
Heading	121/4256 Jan 1915 3 Division 9th Field Ambulance Vol VI		
War Diary	Berthen	01/01/1915	31/01/1915
Heading	121/4508 Feb 1915 9th Field Ambulance Vol VII		
War Diary	Berthen	01/02/1915	28/02/1915
Miscellaneous	Appendix I		
Miscellaneous	Hd Qrs 3 Division		
Miscellaneous	Appendix II	09/02/1915	09/02/1915
Heading	121/4871 March 1915 9th Field Ambulance Vol VIII		
War Diary	Berthen	01/03/1915	21/03/1915
War Diary	Boeschepe	22/03/1915	31/03/1915
War Diary	Berthen	01/03/1915	21/03/1915
Heading	War Diary 9th Field Ambulance 3rd Division Month Of March 1915		
Heading	121/5194 April 1915 9th Field Ambulance Vol IX		
War Diary	Boeschepe	01/04/1915	10/04/1915
Map	Map		
Miscellaneous	O.C. 9th Field Ambulance	11/04/1915	11/04/1915
War Diary	Boeschepe	10/04/1915	11/04/1915
War Diary	Berthen-Westoutre Road	12/04/1915	14/04/1915
Miscellaneous	A Form Messages And Signals		
War Diary	Berthen-Westoutre	15/04/1915	15/04/1915
War Diary	Westoutre	16/04/1915	30/04/1915
Heading	May 1915 3rd Division No.9 Field Ambulance Vol X		
War Diary	Westoutre	01/05/1915	03/05/1915
War Diary	Mt Kokereele	04/05/1915	30/05/1915
War Diary	Boeschepe-Poperinghe Road	31/05/1915	31/05/1915
Heading	3rd Division June 1915 No.9 Field Ambulance Vol XI		
War Diary	Boeschepe-Poperinghe Road	01/06/1915	30/06/1915
War Diary	Asylum Ypres	29/05/1915	29/06/1915
War Diary	Poperinghe	30/06/1915	30/06/1915
War Diary	Asylum Ypres	29/06/1915	29/06/1915
War Diary	Poperinghe	30/06/1915	30/06/1915
Heading	3rd Division July 15 No.9 Field Ambulance Vol XII		
War Diary	Boeschepe-Poperinghe Road	01/07/1915	23/07/1915
War Diary	Ouderdom	24/07/1915	24/07/1915
War Diary	Busseboom-Boeschepe Road	25/07/1915	31/07/1915
War Diary	Farm by Dickebusch Wood	24/07/1915	31/07/1915

W095
1407/2

3RD DIVISION
MEDICAL

NO.9. FIELD AMBULANCE
AUG - DEC 1914.

Confidential

War Diary
of
No. 9 Field Ambulance III Division.

from 5th August 1914 to 31st August 1914.

[signature]
Lt Col Ramb
O.C. No. 9 Field Ambulance

Army Form C. 2118.

WAR DIARY
or
INTELLIGENCE SUMMARY.
(Erase heading not required.)

Instructions regarding War Diaries and Intelligence Summaries are contained in F. S. Regs., Part II. and the Staff Manual respectively. Title pages will be prepared in manuscript.

Hour, Date, Place	Summary of Events and Information	Remarks and references to Appendices
4 p.m. 5-8-14. SOUTHSEA.	LIEUT-COLONEL G.S. McLOUGHLIN (O.C. Unit), MAJOR E.W. BLISS (O.C. "B" Section), MAJOR W.E. HUDLESTON (O.C. "C" Section), CAPT. ROBERTS, LIEUT & MR CONWAY, 2. N.C.O⁂ and 16 men joined. Billet at ROYAL BEACH HOTEL and horses in vicinity. Received two copies of orders and diaries for mobilization, one from A.D.M.S. PORTSMOUTH, one from O.C. No: 6 Coy. These copies not identical in detail; much diverse matter included in copy from A.D.M.S. One man joined. Much office work routine, as laid down, followed.	G.M°L
7 p.m. 6.8.14. SOUTHSEA.	Routine followed as laid down.	G.M°L G.M°L
7 p.m. 7.8.14. SOUTHSEA.	54 men joined. Harness and saddlery drawn, with all horse gear and lotathiery hose, also PIMLICO stores.	G.M°L
7 p.m. 8.8.14. SOUTHSEA.	1 W.O. and 117 other ranks joined. A.S. Corps, less 2 N.C.O's joined.	G.M°L
4 p.m. 9-8-14. SOUTHSEA.	Handed over saddlery, harness and horse gear to A.S.C. Sergeant. CAPT FRASER and the following Officers of Special Reserve. CAPT. HABGOOD, LIEUTS. FISHER and TULLOCH, joined last night. 6 recruits joined. Prepared horse lines on SOUTHSEA Common.	G.M°L G.M°L
4 p.m. 10-8-14. SOUTHSEA.		
4 p.m. 11.8.14. SOUTHSEA.	Stores taken over at COSHAM by CAPT. FRASER and A.S.C. at COSHAM STATION. Arrived in lines prepared at SOUTHSEA Common.	G.M°L

WAR DIARY
or
INTELLIGENCE SUMMARY.
(Erase heading not required.)

Army Form C. 2118.

Hour, Date, Place	Summary of Events and Information	Remarks and references to Appendices
7pm, 11.8.14. SOUTHSEA. (continued)	COMMON at 11 a.m., train being late (due to arrive 12-27am). Fitted and marked saddlery 90. Shoeing commenced. Mobilization reserve of shoes (in unit) had to be drawn on as suitable shoes were not locally available. 160 of the H.Draught collars could not be fitted to any of the horses, exchange, chiefly for partworn collars, need arranged for. Knives, land Yards, billet sleeping and breeder to soreness today. Shoeing, fitting of harness completed, arrangements made to replenish mobilization stock of shoes as far as possible. 1 man sent to HOSPITAL. 6 men joined, and 1 man (15th Hussars) joined as Chaplain's orderly. LIEUT. F.J.T.HORNE, (temporary Commission) joined. Heavy rain last night and today.	Sgd.
4pm, 12-8-14. SOUTHSEA.		Sgd.
7pm, 13-8-14. SOUTHSEA.	Drew remainder of Ordnance Equipment and all medical and veterinary stores. 2 Sergeants A.S.C. joined; these were + are late. late, the sergeant who formerly joined had been unable to cope with his work, the duties (being all reservists) requiring much instruction in their duties.	Sgd.
7pm, 14.8.14. SOUTHSEA.	Two men joined during last night, 1 man sent to hospital	Sgd.

Army Form C. 2118.

WAR DIARY
or
INTELLIGENCE SUMMARY.
(Erase heading not required.)

Instructions regarding War Diaries and Intelligence Summaries are contained in F.S. Regs., Part II. and the Staff Manual respectively. Title pages will be prepared in manuscript.

Hour, Date, Place	Summary of Events and Information	Remarks and references to Appendices
7/am. 14.8.14. SOUTHSEA. (Continued)	Hospital. Mobilisation completed about noon, all vehicles loaded yesterday; many minor adjustments made this morning. Three vehicles damaged by entrained drivers and horses yesterday repaired today. 3 surplus men to No. 6. Coy.	Sgn L
7pm. 15.8.14. SOUTHSEA.	Continued training of men and horses.	Sgn L
7pm. 16.8.14. SOUTHSEA.	Continued training of men and horses.	Sgn L
7pm. 17.8.14. SOUTHSEA.	Continued training men and horses.	Sgn L
7pm. 18.8.14. SOUTHSEA.	Handed over horse details to Lt. Col. GARNER. to be left at base. (directed by A.D.M.S, PORTSMOUTH) Rev^d. B.W. ROWAN. C.F. (attached) joined last night.	Sgn L
9pm 19-8-14 at Sea	1st Trainload paraded at 11·30 p.m. last night, entrained at PORTSMOUTH·TOWN STATION at 1·14 a.m. this morning; train left at 2·40 a.m. (13 minutes late). 2nd Trainload paraded 1/2 midnight 18/19 - 8·14; entrained at 2·45 a.m., train left at 3·45 a.m. 1st. Trainload arrived at SOUTHAMPTON DOCK at 4 a.m. 2nd. Trainload at 5·45 a.m. Both Trainloads entrained	Sgn L

Army Form C. 2118.

WAR DIARY
~~INTELLIGENCE SUMMARY.~~
(Erase heading not required.)

Instructions regarding War Diaries and Intelligence Summaries are contained in F. S. Regs., Part II. and the Staff Manual respectively. Title pages will be prepared in manuscript.

Hour, Date, Place	Summary of Events and Information	Remarks and references to Appendices
9 p.m. 19-8-14. At Sea (Continued)	Embarked during day (ship being late), and sailed at 7-20 p.m. on "ARMERIAN", No. 8 Field Ambulance on same ship.	G.W.C.
9 a.m. 20-8-14. ROUEN.	Arrived at 5 p.m., commenced unloading, men disembarked, also 21 horses. At 8 p.m. disembarkation stopped as cranes ceased working; men re-embarked, horses picketted on Quay. Work of disembarkation slow as vehicles and horses of the two units were mixed on ship; and cranes not suitable for heavy loaded vehicles.	G.W.C.
9 p.m. 21-8-14. ROUEN.	Recommenced disembarkation at 6 a.m., Completed at 12 noon. Reached REST CAMP at MONT ST. AIGNAN at 2-15 p.m.	G.W.C.
7 p.m. 22-8-14. ROUEN.	Remained in REST CAMP.	G.W.C.
7 p.m. 23-8-14. ON MARCH. VALENCIENNES to ST. WAAST.	Commenced entraining at 10 p.m. entrained in about an hour, started at 3-4 a.m. arrived VALENCIENNES at 3-8 p.m. 2 horses lamed by stamping and kicking in train, and left at VALENCIENNES Station, in charge of Railway Staff Officer. De-entrained in about 20 minutes. Communicated with 3rd & 6th 3rd Division through	G.W.C.

WAR DIARY

INTELLIGENCE SUMMARY.
(Erase heading not required.)

Army Form C. 2118.

Instructions regarding War Diaries and Intelligence Summaries are contained in F.S. Regs., Part II. and the Staff Manual respectively. Title pages will be prepared in manuscript.

Hour, Date, Place	Summary of Events and Information	Remarks and references to Appendices
4 pm 23.6.14 (Continued)	through an Officer locally apprehended about 5 pm commenced march for SARS LA BRUYERE to join Division.	order attached.
12 m.n. 24/25.6.14. at Bois LA CRETTE.	Reached ST. WAAST about 12·15 a.m. rested till 3 a.m. then marched and met D.D.M.S. 2nd ARMY CORPS near HON, and received from him instructions to the effect that the unit was not to proceed beyond SARS LA BRUYERE, except under later orders, no partial retirement was in progress, on the march communicated by telephone with 3rd Division 1st Div'n through LIEUT HARRISON. R.I. Regt representative mentioned above who was marching with the unit. Crossed Belgian Frontier sent on Capt ROBERTS to report at Divisional H'Quarters. Action in progress. At 7·45 a.m. received order to return to BAVAI. during retirement at 8·25 a.m. at the DOUANE BELGE received through Capt ROBERTS verbal message to send all ambulance wagons to SARS LA BRUYERE and report to the First O.C. troops met, remainder of Unit to proceed by route HON- HOUDAIN, St WAAST —BERMERIES—	See 2 order attached.

WAR DIARY

INTELLIGENCE SUMMARY.

(Erase heading not required.)

Army Form C. 2118.

Place	Summary of Events and Information	Remarks and references to Appendices
(...ined).	BERMERIES-ANFROIPRET to GOMMEGNIES, and to await orders. Party with Ambulance Wagons comprised Major HUDLESTON, Capt ROBERTS and other ranks, bearer sub-division "C" Section, with water Cart and portion of Medical Equipment. At 10.50am at MON received verbal orders from Staff of 2nd Army Corps (through Major BLISS) to "push on at once to B'WAAST, thence to WARGNIES." Where horses could be watered "Supply Wagons go to temporary Depôt there to unload. Supply Wagons go to temporary Depôt of Supplies and assist to distribute supplies to troops arriving in the Area. Carried out order as far as Warsill, found Supplies at BOIS LA CRETTE, but troops of 3rd Division for whom supplies were intended received only a portion of the supplies.	Report from Major HUDLESTON attached, also one from Capt ROBERTS
...CATEAU.	Assault of Engineers unable to join 9th Infantry Brigade on march, though the night had collected 2 officers and 12 other ranks sick and wounded passing through. Approached by O.C. 1st Bn R.I. Rifles and R.A.M.C. Officer attached (Capt LEWIS) as to supplying Battalion with Medical material, cart and personnel, for watercarts, message attached Supplied one Medical Companion.	

WAR DIARY
INTELLIGENCE SUMMARY
(Erase heading not required.)

Army Form C. 2118.

Instructions regarding War Diaries and Intelligence Summaries are contained in F.S. Regs., Part II. and the Staff Manual respectively. Title pages will be prepared in manuscript.

Hour, Date, Place	Summary of Events and Information	Remarks and references to Appendices
12.n. 4. 25/26-8-14 (Continued)	marched with 9th Infantry Brigade to LE QUESNOY where wounded men sent off by train, here went met Major HUDDESTON Cap't ROBERTS and remainder of party, with the Ambulance wagons, directed by Staff to proceed to SOLESMES, Brigade having moved on. On arrival there met Rear guard (Royal Scots Fusiliers), no information obtainable as to position or route of remainder of Division, ordered out of town by G.O.C. Cavalry Division. Proceeded on own initiative (after considerable trouble in leaving town on account of congestion of traffic) through NEUVILLY (where was great confusion of traffic), to LE CATEAU. Still no news of Division, town was about to be evacuated, noted. (Halted about ½ an hour since)	Gen'l
12.n. 4. 26/27-8-14. On night march to ESTREES.	marched at 2 a.m. to BUISIGN (on own initiative) in order to get information as to whereabouts the 3rd Division, these obtained a few sick and wounded collected during retirement yesterday. Received orders despatch rider from A.D.M.S. to proceed to MARETZ to be in reserve during the action in the neighbourhood. At MARETZ collected several wounded chiefly brought by motors, made a Dressing Station (with "B" Field Ambulance), in a Farm, ordered to retire suddenly, later returned and continued to work, finally retired under orders, and marched for ESTREES. Pickering	Gen'l

WAR DIARY

INTELLIGENCE SUMMARY.

Army Form C. 2118.

Hour, Date, Place	Summary of Events and Information	Remarks and references to Appendices
12.n.n. 26/27-8-14 (continued)	picking up a few more wounded by the way. Received three contradictory orders (verbally) at ESTREES, finally started for night march in column of wheeled vehicles for unknown destination. On confusion, left behind Major HUDLESTON, Capt HABGOOD with other personnel, and vehicles. LIEUT. TULLOCH with one Ambulance wagon who attempted to entrain sick on march has not yet rejoined; all the above are presumably following in the Column.	G.L.
11 p.m. 27-8-14 outside HAM.	Rested for 2 hours during last night, marched by St QUENTIN to DURY where unit was ordered to go into Billets by Staff 2nd Army Corps, after this was arranged unit was ordered to go on and cross river, went on to HAM, rested outside at 4 am.	G.L.
11 p.m. 28-8-14 ~~Pont~~ VARESNES.	Turned out at 2am. and marched to GUISCARD thence to NOYON, where wounded were placed in charge of a Rest station party for entrainment, marched by PONTOISE, at which place the Staff at NOYON informed me that the 3rd Division would be billeted, on arrival at PONTOISE learnt that 3rd Division went at VARESNES, to which place the unit proceeded and Bivouacked	G.L.

Army Form C. 2118.

WAR DIARY
INTELLIGENCE SUMMARY.
(Erase heading not required.)

Instructions regarding War Diaries and Intelligence Summaries are contained in F.S. Regs., Part II. and the Staff Manual respectively. Title pages will be prepared in manuscript.

Hour, Date, Place	Summary of Events and Information	Remarks and references to Appendices
11 p.m. 29-8-1914. On march CUTTS — VIC-SUR-AISNE.	Marched in afternoon to CUTTS there bivouacked and were joined by Major HUDLESTON, Capt HABGOOD, other personnel and vehicles. At 8.30pm received verbal orders from Divisional Staff to move to VIC-SUR-AISNE, marched at 9.30pm, with the 7 and 8 Field Ambulances and artillery.	Gn.k
11 p.m. 30-8-1914. LE CHAT EMBARRASSÉ.	Passed through VIC-SUR-AISNE and went into bivouac here	Gn.k Gn.k
11 p.m. 31-8-1914. VAUCIENNES.	At 3.45am marched in company with the 7 and 8 Field Ambulances by "FERME DE POUY" — MORTEFONTAINE — TAILLEFONTAINE — EMEVILLE by CREPY (where the original order was to bivouac) to VAUCIENNES, where unit bivouacked in the 9th Infantry Brigade area.	

SECRET.
EXPEDITIONARY FORCE.
RAILWAY TIME TABLES.

9877(A).
1-3-13.
Recd 25/2/14
GSR

9th Field Ambulance

Train Number	Division	Brigade	Designating Letter	UNIT	Officers	Other Ranks	Officers' Chargers / Other Horses / Heavy Draught	Guns and Description	Vehicles 4 Wheel	Vehicles 2 Wheel	Bicycles	Baggage and Stores Tons	FROM	Day	Time	Firsts	Composite	Thirds	Horse Boxes	Cattle Trucks	Small	Large	Van Trucks	Drop-sided Wagons	Baggage Vans	Brake Vehicles	Total Number of Vehicles	Contracting Railway Company	Remarks
X1104	3rd			9. Fd Ambulance	½ 5	195	17/21		10	2	1		Portsmouth Town	11.3.	Oxygen at 2:15. 2.21 AM		1	2		5	11					2	21	L S W Ry	
X1105	-"-			-"-	½ 5	100	14/18		8	4			-"-	11.3.	Oxyg. at 2-45 3.45 AM 2.45?		1	2		6	10				2	2	21	-"-	
30	-"-			-"-		18						2½	Cosham	14.3.	2 P.M													-"-	Details Ry

O.C. 9th Field Ambulance

Return at once to
BAVAI

Aeroplane
main route
BAVAI

24/8/14

(Received by motor cycle messenger
from short of Sens la Bruyere
at 1.45 a.m. Apt.)

3rd Division.

For use during the concentration period.
Exécution de la concentration.

DETRAINMENT AND BILLETING ORDER.
ORDRE DE MOUVEMENT PAR VOIE DE TERRE.

Serial number / N° de fractionnement		Remarks. / Observations.
Unit / Indication de l'élément	9th Fd Amb.	
Detraining station / Gare de débarquement	VALENCIENNES	H.Q. 3rd Div
Route (temporary billets underlined). / Itinéraire (gîtes soulignés)	via MARLY – SAULTAIN – JENLAIN – BAVAI – HON –	NOIRCHAIN. Tel N° 188
Final billets / Cantonnement à occuper	SARS LA BRUYERE &	
Billets occupied by / Emplacement — Immediate Superior to whom to report / de l'autorité immédiatement supérieure.	CUESMES	MONS
Other portions of unit. / des autres sub-divisions de l'unité.		

SUPPLY AND EVACUATION OF SICK.
Ravitaillement et Evacuations.

Railhead for supplies / Gare de ravitaillement	LE CATEAU	Issue of order / Remise de l'ordre — Place / Lieu, Date / Date, Hour / Heure
Hour of issue of supplies / Distribution à la G. Rav		

M.L.L. Harrison Lt
Billeting Officer.
L'officier de cantonnement.

for A.A. & Q.M.G 3rd Div

NOTES.

1. At the detraining station—
   (a.) The "Commissaire Militaire (de la Gare)," who is in charge *inside* the station, will issue, to British troops, through the medium of the British detraining officer, all instructions regarding detrainment.
   (b.) The British detraining officer, who is in charge *outside* the station, will issue all instructions regarding assembly places and other arrangements, and about billets if the unit is to stop the night in the locality.
   In all cases the unit must clear the roads from the station and move outside the town as soon as possible, if it is not to be billeted there.
2. The instructions contained in this order (billets, routes, temporary halting places, &c.) must be strictly observed.

OBSERVATIONS IMPORTANTES.

1°. Au point de débarquement, s'adresser :—
   (a.) Pour tout ce qui concerne les débarquements, au "Commissaire militaire" (de la gare) qui exerce les fonctions de commandant d'armes à l'intérieur de la gare.
   (b.) Pour les consignes relatives au stationnement, pour le cantonnement (si l'élément doit passer la nuit dans la localité) et pour tous autres renseignements utiles, à l'officier remplissant les fonctions de commandant d'armes en dehors de la gare.
   Dans tous les cas, avoir soin de dégager le plus tôt possible les routes aux abords de la gare et tenir la troupe en dehors de la localité, si elle ne doit pas y cantonner.
2°. Les indications portées sur le présent ordre (cantonnement, itinéraires, gîtes d'étape s'il y a lieu, etc.) doivent être strictement observées.

(B257) 6050 7/13 H&S 327wo

"A" Form.
Army Form C. 2121.
MESSAGES AND SIGNALS.

Prefix	Code	m.	Words	Charge	This message is on a/c of:	Recd. at	m.
Office of Origin and Service Instructions.			Sent At	m.	Service.	Date	
			To By		(Signature of "Franking Officer.")	From By	

TO — All units (9: F? Ambce)

| Sender's Number | Day of Month | In reply to Number | AAA |
| B.M. 15 | 31st Augt | | |

Troops will be ready to move at 5 a.m.

From 9: I.B.
Place
Time 10.50 p.m.

W Delano Bhnl
Captain
B.M. 9: 2: Bde

The above may be forwarded as now corrected. (Z)

Censor. Signature of Addressor or person authorised to telegraph in his name.

* This line should be erased if not required.

MESSAGES AND SIGNALS. "A" Form. Army Form C. 2121.

TO: OC 9th Fd Ambulance

I have lost my Maltese cart will you supply me with a medical companion & two orderlies for my water carts I would also like a medical & surgical panniers & a maltese cart could also be supplied my regiment has had long marches & I consider it essential that a cart be supplied if possible

From: O.C. Irish Rifles
Time: 7.55 p.m.

Signature: W.D. Bird Lt Col

MESSAGES AND SIGNALS.

"A" Form.

Prefix	Code	Words	Charge	This message is on a/c of	Recd. at
					Date
Office of Origin and Service Instructions.	Sent At ... m. To ... By		Service (Signature of "Franking Officer.")	From By	

TO — O.C. 9th Fld Ambulance

Sender's Number.	Day of Month	In reply to Number		AAA
51	31. 8. 14			

Following message received from A.H.Qrs begins indents for medical stores required by Field Ambulances should be made for the present on No.1. base medical stores A.A.A. No 2 base supply of dressings should arrive by supply trains 29th and 30th inst.

From: MEDICAL
Place: VAUNNOISE
Time:

Major RAMC

"A" Form.
MESSAGES AND SIGNALS.

Army Form C. 2121

Prefix	Code	m.	Words	Charge			Recd. at	m.
Office of Origin and Service Instructions.			Sent		This message is on a/c of:		Date	
			At	m.		Service.	From	
			To					
			By		(Signature of "Franking Officer.")		By	

TO {

Sender's Number	Day of Month	In reply to Number	**A A A**

4. Order of march			
Unit	To pass Crossroads immediately W of Sugar Refinery.	Starting Points VANNOISE STATION	
48th Heavy Battery	9.15	9.40	
57th Fd Coy RE	9.25	9.50	
9th Fd Amb.	9.30	9.55	
23rd FA Bde (less 1 Batty)	9.35	10 am	
1st Line R.	9.50	10.15	
1st R S Fus.	9.55	10.20	
Div H Q.		10.25	
5. Rearguard Commander Brig Genl F C Shaw C.B.			
4/R Fus. 4/North Fus. 1 Batty 23rd Bde RFA Divl Mounted Troops	} To rendezvous at 1000 yds North of VAUCIENNES at 6.45 am		

From
Place
Time

The above may be forwarded as now corrected. (Z)
Censor. Signature of Addressee or person authorised to telegraph in his name.

"A" Form
MESSAGES AND SIGNALS.

Prefix	Code	m	Words	Charge	This message is on a/c of:	Recd. at	m
Office of Origin and Service Instructions.						Date	
			Sent At	m		From	
			To		Service.		
			By		(Signature of "Franking Officer.")	By	

TO

| Sender's Number | Day of Month | In reply to Number | AAA |

6. Outposts

The 4/R Scots mo will continue to hold the outpost line till 7 am after which hour they will concentrate near the Bde Starting Point.

Issued 5.30 am

McClaw Spmr Capt

Copy No 1 — 4 R 7 mo
     2 — " Nmt mo
     3 — " Linc R
     4 — " R S mo
     5 — 57th 70 Coy RE
     6 — 231st Bde RFA
     7 — H my Batt
     8 — 4 R 70 amb

From
Place
Time

The above may be forwarded as now corrected. (Z)

Censor. Signature of Addressor or person authorised to telegraph in his name.

* This line should be erased if not required.

O.C 9th Fd Amb.

Colonel Stone has asked me to inform you that your Brigade area is VAUCIENNES.

S E Fielding
Major R.A.M.C
O.C. No.7 Fd Amb.

Mermont
31-8-14
4-30pm.

"C" Form (Original). Army Form C. 2123.
MESSAGES AND SIGNALS.

TO: 9th Fd Amb

DIV will be ready to move southwards at 3.30 am

FROM: 9th INF BDE

TIME: 10 hrs

9th Fd Amb

"A" Form.   Army Form C. 2121.
MESSAGES AND SIGNALS.

TO	ALL	UNITS	
Sender's Number	Day of Month	In reply to Number	**A A A**

Cancel previous message AAA
DIV ready to move 2.30
am

From: 9th INF BDE
Place:
Time: 10.40

Secret

O.C. No 9. Field Ambulance
___

Please note that your unit will proceed from Portsmouth Town Station on Wednesday next the 19th inst in two halves 1st at 2.21 am by train X112̊ 2nd at 3.45 am by train X1105.

No officer available

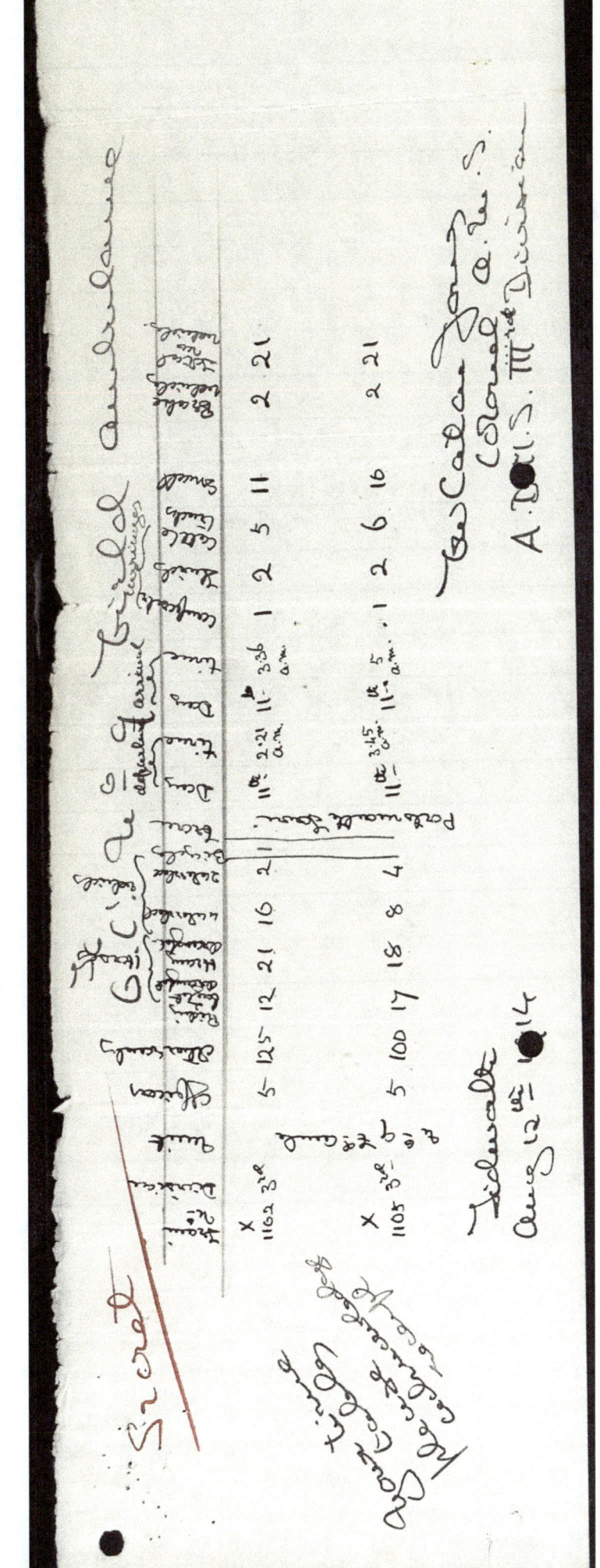

War Diary
of
No. 9 Field Ambulance.
(C. Section)

Aug 1914

24 Aug	Marched via BAVAY – HON – to
5 am	within 1½ miles of SARS LA BRUYERE
10 am	Hot action going on in direction of EUGIES – FRAMERIES. Orders received from a G.S. officer 2nd Army as follows :- The 10 ambulance wagons to be detached, and sent with a Medical Officer to SARS LA BRUYERE, the officer to report himself to the OC troops at that place. The remainder of the q.f. Amb to march back by a specified route to GOMMEGNIES. MAJOR HUDLESTON ordered to carry out the orders as regards Ambulance Wagons. The wagons with wagon orderlies, and reserve dressing boxes detached, also the bearer sub division of "C" Section & the transport sergt of C Section. Capt Roberts joined us en route.
11 AM	Arrived SARS LA BRUYERE and parked ambulance wagons off main street. Rode forward about a mile and found Genl HAKING who ordered me to remain in SARS LA BRUYERE ready to retire at any moment as the place would probably be shelled, our troops in full retreat along line SARS LA BRUYERE – BLARGNIES A few wounded brought back and taken over
12 Noon	Met a G.S. officer of Inf Bde who had bicycled in from BLARGNIES he stated that

medical assistance was badly required at that place – I therefore moved on to BLARGNIES, Capt Roberts leading the wagons whilst I rode & reported to ADMS COL CATON JONES, the position of No 9 F amb as above noted. He reported to GOC II Div, and ordered me to fill up my ambulance wagons with wounded quickly.

2 PM Seven ambulance wagons 4 full & 3 empty ordered back to MALPLAQUET by main road leading S.W. 3 ambulance wagons remained behind with me.

4 PM Having picked up some more wounded ordered to proceed back by route BLARESGNIES – 3rd class road S of RIEU de BARY – B of B S de BLAREGNIES – Cross road S of LA CHAUSSEE DU BOIS – CAMP PERDU to MALPLAQUET – Having reached the cross roads last mentioned, was ordered straight back to HON by a GS officer, and was thus cut off from my other ambulance wagons. Halted at cross road immediately N of N of HON and picked up all wounded who passed, the troops chiefly III D Div being in full retreat on BAVAY. Sent message attached by motor cyclist orderly to OC No 9 F Amb.

24 Aug

8 PM The last of infantry having apparently
passed, returned on BAVAY. The entrance to
the town was quite blocked with troops, but was
allowed through as I was carrying wounded.
Arrived in centre of town found HdQrs 2nd army
and inquired of any hospital accommodation
for my wounded. and was directed to a
Convent near by but the Sisters could not take
them. Found an improvised Red Cross hospital
where the serious cases were accommodated
in bed & remainder on straw & hay.
Left below named at this hospital

No	Name	Corps	Wounds etc
39164	G. Low	49 By RFA	Gunshot left knee Severe
6708	Pte Carter E	2 S Lancs	Gunshot right elbow joint V. Severe
882	Pte Holywood	15 Hussars	Sprain left knee & shoulder
8622	Pte Johnson	5 Lancs	Sprain of back
10333	Pte Knight	Worcester R[egt]	Slipped cartilage knee
41586	Dr Wray	30 By, Ammn Col	Wound rt shoulder shrapnel (slight)
64602	Dr Chambers	49 By RFA	Wound head Slight
1113	Pte Ritchie	Gordon Highrs	Gunshot wound ankle slight

No	Name	Corps	Wounds
8803	Pte Inglis	2 R Scots Fus	Dislocated Shoulder
8829	Pte Bell	do	Gunshot wound rt Knee
8231	Pte Layton W		Wound elbow shell (slight)
28332	Dr GARR	49 By RFA	Wound Shoulder Shell (slight)
7586	Pte Parrot	Lincoln Reg	Gunshot rt elbow (Severe)
7901	Pte Brakespear	"	" Scalp slight
10140	Pte Pratt	R I Reg	" left forearm (Severe)
7813	Pte Clark	Lincoln	" Scalp Slight
11377	Pte Lawrence	R Fus	Sprain ankle left

25 Aug

1. AM Again tried to get into touch with my unit through HdQrs 2nd Army, but was told the wire was broken. Eventually was shewn route by which the 3rd Div would march. Horses & men exhausted so remained night at BAVAY

6 AM marched via BERMERIES – AMFROIPRET – GOMMEGNIES – VILLEREAU – to LE QUESNOY Picked up Capt Roberts with the other 7 ambulance wagons at GOMMEGNIES. He had retained the wounded picked up by him yesterday

11 AM. Reached Rly. Station at Lebresnoy and loaded up all wounded, and sick on a train waiting there, waggon floors covered with hay — No personnel sent with them, but water-bottles were filled, and a Sick Soldier who had been a hospital orderly in India placed in charge of the serious cases. Many other cases were loaded on this train, as a GS officer present stated that all men capable of standing but unable to march were to be sent down.

12 Noon. The remainder of the F Amb arrived & we joined up.

A. Hodleston
Major RAMC
OC "C" Section
Roy F Amb

24th. August 1914.
    Blaregnies, Belgium.
Received orders from Major Huddleston R.A.M.C. to proceed, with seven Ambulance Wagons containing 8 lying down Wounded & 8 sitting up, to Bavai & to report to O.C no 7 or 8 Field Ambulance. On arrival at Bavai about 4 p.m. reported to O.C no 7 Field Ambulance who gave me instructions to transfer the wounded to the Civil Hospital & then proceed along the Bermeries, Amfroipret, Gommegnies Road to join up with his Ambulance Wagons which would be left on the Road.
The Civil Hospital could not take the wounded unless dressings & an M.O were left to look after them so I proceeded to join no 7 Field Ambulance retaining the wounded.
I joined no 7 F.A about 9 pm &

meet with Major Fielding RAMC + 10 Amb: Wagons to Bivouac at Bermenies.

25th August 1914.
Proceeded with Amb: Wagons of No 4 Field Ambulance in the direction of Le Quesnoy + at Gommegnies joined Major Huddleston RAMC with 3 Amb: Wagons + proceed under his orders to Le Quesnoy where Wounded were transferred to an Ambulance Train + at this Station joined No 9 Field Ambulance who were passing through.

Fred Roberts
Capt RAMC.

AMD

WAR DIARY
No 9 Field Ambulance.
Volume 4

12/1058
Sept. 1914

Army Form C. 2118.

WAR DIARY
INTELLIGENCE SUMMARY.
(Erase heading not required.)

Instructions regarding War Diaries and Intelligence Summaries are contained in F.S. Regs., Part II. and the Staff Manual respectively. Title pages will be prepared in manuscript.

Hour, Date, Place	Summary of Events and Information	Remarks and references to Appendices
11 p.m. 1-9-1914. BOUILLANCY.	Marched with 9th Infantry Brigade through LEVIGNEN by FRESNOY & VILLERS to BOUILLANCY where the Unit bivouacked in 9th Infantry Brigade area. Captains FRASER and HABGOOD with 2 ambulance wagons were, under orders of A.D.M.S. dropped with other personnel at LEVIGNEN, the personnel at 9 p.m. transferred sick and wounded to Motor Lorries. Lieut TULLOCH and the Rev. ROWAN C.F. rejoined.	Apl (Order attached.)
11 p.m. 2-9-1914. LESCHES.	Left Bivouac 4.30 a.m. Marched by FOSSE MARTIN — DOUY — MARCILLY — BARCY to PENCHARD. Halted till 6.15 p.m. when orders were received from A.D.M.S. to march at 6.30 p.m. less 3 ambulance wagons left behind (with Capt FRASER and other personnel) to LESCHES, in company with No 7 and 8 Field Ambulances under command of Lieut Col. STONE, arrived at LESCHES at 10.45 p.m. Early in the afternoon Lieut FISHER detailed for attachment to 9ooth? Invaliders and Lieut TULLOCH for Royal Scots Invaliders; sick and wounded transferred to Motor Lorries.	Apl (Order attached?)
11 p.m. 3-9-1914. LA LOGE ARTVS.	Marched at 7.15 a.m. under verbal orders transmitted by A.D.V.S. to proceed to PERE LEVEE. Route by ESBLY — MONTRY — COUILLY — CRECY, long halt at 11.30 a.m. Instructions having been received from Acting Staff Officer	Apl

WAR DIARY
INTELLIGENCE SUMMARY.
(Erase heading not required.)

Army Form C. 2118

Hour, Date, Place	Summary of Events and Information	Remarks and references to Appendices
1 pm 3-9-1914	(Continued) that orders for march had been altered, remained halted awaiting further orders. At 5 pm orders received (through officer despatched to Divisional Headquarters) that unit was to proceed to LE MANS farm where 9th Infantry Brigade H.Q. were established: this was found to be incorrect, Brigade H.Q. being actually at LA LOGE ARTUS: here we bivouacked, finding Capt FRASER and party complete	[signature]
11 pm 4-9-14. On march	At 7 am ordered to be in readiness to move at short notice, marched at 1.30 pm independently, acting on verbal Brigade orders (received at 1.15 pm), to point at which road LA HAUTE MAISON – CRECY crosses main road SANCY – VOISINS. Remained there till about 3 pm, ordered (verbally) on to MONPERTHS. Received order (attached) prepared to move at 10.30 pm via CRECY. Received at 10-20 pm operation order No. 8 by Brigade Commander. Marched at 10-30 pm.	[signature]
11 pm 5-9-14 CHÂTRES	Went into Bivouac outside CHÂTRES about 7 a.m. Route followed was CRECY – crossroads ½ mile south of BESSY Ch. – crossroads ½ mile N.W. of B. of BELLEVUE CH. (order attached 3)	[signature] (order attached 3)

WAR DIARY

INTELLIGENCE SUMMARY.

(Erase heading not required.)

Army Form C. 2118.

Hour, Date, Place	Summary of Events and Information	Remarks and references to Appendices
11 pm. 5-9-14 (continued).	OBELISQUE. Followed 1st Royal Scots Fusiliers but order of march was broken by 1st reinforcements being brought into Column just ahead of the unit. These men were very fatigued and threw away much of their kit on the march. Many sick and exhausted picked up on march. No objective of clearance has been given; handed over sick to train wagon in anticipation of there meeting the motor lorries.	[signature]
11 pm. 6-9-14 LUMIGNY.	Received Brigade operation order no 25 (attached) Unit in main body. Last unit (following 57 My R.F) to Two starting point at 7·40 am, Route CHAMPROSE FARM - CH LA HOUSSAYE. Reached LUMIGNY and went into bivouac outside at 7pm. Had picked up several wounded from Cavalry Division en route, also several sick & exhausted men.	[signature] (Order attached 4.)
11 pm. 7/9/14 LE MARTROY	Marched by COULOMMIERS where an ambulance train was found, entrained sick and wounded and went on to LE MARTROY	[signature]

WAR DIARY
INTELLIGENCE SUMMARY.
(Erase heading not required.)

Army Form C. 2118

Instructions regarding War Diaries and Intelligence Summaries are contained in F.S. Regs., Part II. and the Staff Manual respectively. Title pages will be prepared in manuscript.

Hour, Date, Place	Summary of Events and Information	Remarks and references to Appendices
11pm 8-9-1914 ORLY	Marched by road REBAIS - ORLY - BUSSIERES (orders notified CITRY as end of march), fighting and collecting of wounded from GIBRALTAR onwards, collected several wounded.	(Order Attached 5.)
11pm 9-9-1914 BEZU.	Marched through the night 8/9-9-14 and halted north of BUSSIERES to attend to wounded and endeavour to clear by means of motor lorries; but as lorries were not available went on LES FOUCHERES arriving about 2 p.m. Cleared by supply lorries about 6 p.m., 3 Ambulance wagons and tense subdivision of "C" Section with O.C. unit went on with Brigade remainder followed to Cross roads between SAACY and CITRY. Advanced party shelled about PLATRIERES: went on in evening to BEZU. C.O. went back to Cross roads brought up remainder of heavier and ambulance wagons with me following Cart and followed to BEZU here collected nearly 200 wounded, chiefly from 5th Division, and Retirement	(Order attached 6.)

Army Form C. 2118.

WAR DIARY
INTELLIGENCE SUMMARY.
(Erase heading not required.)

Instructions regarding War Diaries and Intelligence Summaries are contained in F. S. Regs., Part II. and the Staff Manual respectively. Title pages will be prepared in manuscript.

Hour, Date, Place	Summary of Events and Information	Remarks and references to Appendices
11 p.m. 9-9-14. (Continued)	Lieutenant CARBERRY and Lieutenant ELKINGTON. (Temporary Commission) joined.	G.n'L
11 p.m. 10-9-14. DAMMARD.	Last night worked through night with wounded, sent back 120 slighter cases by lorries this morning at 5 a.m., marched about midday, leaving Lieuts CARBERRY and ELKINGTON with aid men in charge of wounded. Marched by NEUILLY LA POTERIE where wounded were collected by our advanced bearer subdivision with wagons and other field ambulances. Several wounded. Left Major BLISS and Lieut. THORNE with that subdivision of "B" Section (who had joined with remainder of unit about 11 a.m.) here and marched to this place by CHEZY. Heavy rain.	G.n'L
11 p.m. 11-9-14. GRAND-ROZOY.	Heavy rain through day. Marched by NEUILLY - OULCHY (la ville) Major BLISS, Lieut THORNE and "B" Sect subdivision joined. †	(Order attached 7-) G.n'L
11 a.m. 12-9-14. BRAINE.	Just arrived after hard march in rain. Capt. FRASER marched ahead (with Brigade) with B Bearer Sub Division and Ambulance wagons and forage cart.	G.n'L

WAR DIARY
INTELLIGENCE SUMMARY.
(Erase heading not required.)

Army Form C. 2118

Hour, Date, Place	Summary of Events and Information	Remarks and references to Appendices
11 p.m. 13.9.1914. BRAINE.	Waited through day, help to collect many sick and wounded (including Germans) into a local French Voluntary Aid Hospital. Awaited orders for advance all day. Capt. HABGOOD with "C" Bearer Subdivision in advance with Brigade. (first returned). Lieuts CARBERRY and ELKINGTON with Party rejoined.	Gen.
11.p.m 14.9.14. BRAINE.	Formed Dressing Station with "B" Section. Sent Subdivision in French Hospital at BRAINE. Marched out remainder of unit (order attached.)	Gen.
11.p.m 15.9.14. BRAINE.	Last night marched by BRENELLE (A.D.M.S. accompanied unit most of the way), left all vehicles except ambulance wagons 1 watercart, and 1 medical Store cart at BRENELLE and proceeded to bridge go at VAILLY. A pontoon bridge had been constructed and the permanent bridge sufficiently repaired to allow of foot traffic; pontoon approaches impassable for vehicles. Went into VAILLY with bearers and 2 ambulances of "A" & "C" Sections and brought over a large number of wounded collected by Regimental medical establishments in the village. Loaded	Gen.

WAR DIARY
INTELLIGENCE SUMMARY.
(Erase heading not required.)

Army Form C. 2118

Instructions regarding War Diaries and Intelligence Summaries are contained in F. S. Regs., Part II. and the Staff Manual respectively. Title pages will be prepared in manuscript.

Hour, Date, Place	Summary of Events and Information	Remarks and references to Appendices
11 pm. 15.9.14. BRAINE. (Continued)	loaded up wagons and returned to BRAINE in early morning, bringing in party left at BRENELLE. Night attack made on Brigade about 11 p.m. last night while wagons were being loaded. Tent under desultory shell fire armed at Bridge and road, 5 officers and 59 other ranks (wounded) placed in Franco-British ambulance train (temporarily commanded by Major ADYE-CURRAN) during the early morning. Through the day "C" tent subdivision opened in BRAINE. In afternoon proceeded with a tent sub-division, the heavier subdivisions and ambulance wagons by CHASSEMY to bridge at VAILLY. Ambulance wagons moved later at an to. Collected wounded from VAILLY through night. Placed wounded in "B" Section dressing station.	Sh L
11 pm. 16.9.14. BRAINE.	Repeated evening collection from VAILLY last night, wounded to be placed in dressing station, orders received to march out again this evening to collect. One ambulance wagon to collecting wounded from vicinity of BRENELLE.	(Orders attached?) Sh L.

WAR DIARY

INTELLIGENCE SUMMARY.

(Erase heading not required.)

Army Form C. 2118

Hour, Date, Place	Summary of Events and Information	Remarks and references to Appendices
11pm. 17.9.14. BRAINE.	Orders of yesterday carried out, similar collection ordered for this evening; wounded to be placed in No: 4 Clearing Hospital, wagons working each day to help to clear the Clearing Hospital to Railway.	GMcL (order attached 10).
11pm. 18.9.14. BRAINE.	Orders of yesterday carried out, similar orders for night are being carried out, only 8 wounded remain to be removed from VAILLY tonight in our wagons, since.	GMcL
11pm. 19.9.14. BRAINE.	Orders of yesterday carried out. Orders for similar collection tonight, but verbally cancelled by DADMS.	GMcL (order attached 11)
11pm. 20.9.14 BRAINE.	All Bearers and Ambulance wagons marched out after dusk with similar detachments of No's Y and 8 Field Ambulances (the whole under the Command of Lieut-Colonel McLoughlin), to clear Dressing Stations at VAILLY. (about 300 wounded reported).	(order attached) GMcL
11pm. 21.9.14. BRAINE.	"B" and "C" Dressing Stations filled last night, "B" Section Dressing Station cleared through the day to Ambulance train at dusk, "B" and "C" sections marched with all A A Ambulance wagons at dusk, and Bearer Sub Division of "A" Section, to clear above and relieve party	GMcL

WAR DIARY

INTELLIGENCE SUMMARY.

(Erase heading not required.)

Army Form C. 2118

Hour, Date, Place	Summary of Events and Information	Remarks and references to Appendices
11 p.m. 21.9.14 (Continued)	Party of No. 8 Field Ambulance in VAILLY. "B" Section sent Subdivision to take over Dressing Station of "C" Section in BRAINE and cleared to an Ambulance train by motor wagon.	G.W.C.
11 p.m. 22.9.14 BRAINE.	45 wounded (very severe cases) and sick brought in by Ambulance wagons and "B" Bearer Subdivision through the night; all wounded and sick cleared in forenoon to Ambulance train and Clearing Hospital. Bearers of "A" Section (under Capt ROBERTS) formed part of body under command of Lieut-Col KENNEDY (order attached) (O.C. 7 F.A.) for clearing Advanced Dressing Stations at VAILLY, marched at 6 p.m. Ambulance wagons, Gen one conveying supplies and technical material, stopped by verbal order of A.D.M.S. as report had arrived showing few casualties in Advanced Dressing Station.	G.W.C.

WAR DIARY

INTELLIGENCE SUMMARY.
(Erase heading not required.)

Army Form C. 2118.

Hour, Date, Place	Summary of Events and Information	Remarks and references to Appendices
11.30 pm. 23-9-14. BRAINE.	Collected wounded and sick at VAILLY this evening.	SMcL
11 pm. 24-9-14. BRAINE.	"B" and "C" Sections ordered in from VAILLY, relieved by No 16 Field Ambulance. Houses for Dressing Station in RUE DE MARTROY (formerly occupied by "C" Section), handed over to No.5 Clearing Hospital.	SMcL
11 pm. 25-9-14. BRAINE.	"B" and "C" Sections to COURCELLES. Major BLISS in medical and sanitary charge of that village; a house taken for a Dressing Station at COURCELLES	SMcL
11 pm. 26-9-14. BRAINE.	No none.	SMcL SMcL
11 pm. 27-9-14. BRAINE.	No none.	SMcL
11 pm. 28-9-14. BRAINE.	Bearer Subdivision of "A" Section aided in collecting wounded at VAILLY this evening.	SMcL
11 pm. 29-9-14. BRAINE.	Horse and Ambulance wagons moved out of the town into a field.	SMcL

Army Form C. 2118

WAR DIARY
INTELLIGENCE SUMMARY.
(Erase heading not required.)

Instructions regarding War Diaries and Intelligence Summaries are contained in F. S. Regs., Part II. and the Staff Manual respectively. Title pages will be prepared in manuscript.

Hour, Date, Place	Summary of Events and Information	Remarks and references to Appendices
11 pm 30.9.14. BRAINE	O.C. unit with tenner sub-divn and ambulance wagons of "A" and "B" Sections collected wounded and sick from VAILLY after dusk.	Diary from Major BLISS. R.A.M.C. received today, attached.

G.M.C.
Lt Colonel R.A.M.C.
O.C. No. 9 F. Ambulance

Head quarters 3rd Division

The O.C.
9th Fld Ambulance

By order of the D.D.M.S.
2nd Corps every case is
to be evacuated from
VAILLY tonight including
those unfit for transport.

BRAINE
19/9/14

A Cuthbering
Major
D.A.D.M.S.

Head Qrs 3rd Division
O.C.
9 Field Ambulance

All the Ambulance Waggons of No 7, 8 & 9 Field Ambulances will proceed to the River to-day in the following order
No 7 at 6 o'clock
No 8 at 6.45
No 9 at 7.30 — to follow — the supply waggons of their respective Bds.

BRAINE
19/9/14

A Crookshank
Major
Pamp
ADMS

Cancelled verbally by DADMS at 5 p.m.

Wt. W1154/2240. 7/11. 7,500,000. Sch. 4a.	"A" Form.			Army Form 2121.	
MESSAGES AND SIGNALS.				No. of Message	
Prefix......Code......m.	Words	Charge	This message is on a/c of:	Recd. at......m.	
Office of Origin and Service Instructions.				Date......	
	Sent		......Service.	From......	
	At......m. To...... By......		(Signature of "Franking Officer.")	By......	

TO OCs 7th 8th & 9th Fd Ambula

Sender's Number	Day of Month	In reply to Number	AAA
M 101	17/9/14		

Arrangements for evacuation of casualties from VAILLY tonight are the same as last night except that the supply trains move in order 8th 9th & 7th aaa. The first at 6pm second at 7pm third at 8pm.

From ADMS 3rd Division
Place BRAINE
Time

Col ADMS 3rd Div

O.C. 9th Fd Ambulance
                    BRAINE

You should attempt to reach
the 9th Bde with your whole
unit as opportunities permit
The dressing station will be
at BRAINE

2.10 pm   [signature]
No 6/11   Col AMS
                           ADMS 3rd Dn

Rec'd
15.9.14

O.C.   ⑨   3rd Div H.Q.

No. 9 Field Ambulance

On receipt of this order Nos 7
& 9 Field Ambulances will send
their personnel (less the tent
subdivisions of No. 9 Field Ambulance doing duty at the
Dressing Station at BRAINE) across
the bridge at VAILLY to collect
wounded of the Infantry Bde
on the N bank of the river.
At dusk the Ambulance
Waggons of No 7. 8. 9 Field
Ambulances are to be sent by
the direct road BRAINE —
CHASSEMY — VAILLY to remain
parked S of the river to receive
casualties brought in by personnel
Dressing Station BRAINE.
Removal of wounded to be
continued all night or until the
field is cleared
BRENELLE   A Chadburn
A.S.S.O.M.   D.D.M.S. 3rd Div

41

16-9-16

O.C.
9th Fd Ambulance

Ref attached. Please detach an ambulance waggon with med¹ Officer & necessary personnel to proceed along the BRENELLE Road & join you at CHASSEMY picking up these cases on the way. The Officer should enquire

Copy Operation Orders 9th Bde
11-9-14

1. Results of yesterdays operations includes the capture of 600 prisoners 6 guns and some machine guns. They belonged to the 3rd & 9th German corps and 9th Cavalry Div. The French in spite of heavy losses are advancing with confidence on our right and left
 The 3rd Div. marches today by DAMMARD NEULLY-VICHEL OULCHY LAVILLE-GRAND ROZOY

2. The order of march.

Unit	To pass starting pt Rd Junction 200 yards NORTH of LE CHATEAU.
1 Linc Reg	7-15
R. Sc. Fus	7-20
North'd Fus	7-25
Ry Fus.	7-30
23 Bde FA	7-35
30 Bde	7-50
57 Coy RE	8-5
Sub section Fd amb	8-10

3. The 48th Heavy Batty will join 7th Bde area in accordance with attached 3rd Div orders. Bde amm cols follow 8th Bde area and Fd amb follow ~~Bde~~ ~~cols~~ amm. cols.

4. Reports to Lincoln Reg.

Issued 4:50 am C D Larkin Lieut.
for B.M.

O.C.   6

No. 9 Field Ambulance.

Bring forward your
Bearer Subdivisions and
Ambulance wagons and
proceed to BEZU Village.

A Crokprin(?)
Major R.A.M.C
D.A.D.M.S

1.15 P.M.

9/9/14

"A" Form.
Army Form 2121.

MESSAGES AND SIGNALS.

TO: Operation Order No 17

Sender's Number: 5A 57
Day of Month: 8-9-14

AAA

1. The Div will march today by the road RE BAIS (western boundary only) — ORLY - BUSSIERES - CITRY

2. On our right the first corps uses the road RE BAIS (Eastern boundary) — TRETOIRE — BOITRON — PAYANT — NOGENT

3. On our left the 5th Div uses the road BOISSY - DOVE - ST CYR ST OUEN — SAACY

From: 3 Div

2/ Bn ready in Order of march
Units to pass starting point road junction ½
       N of CHATRES

       NORTH'D FUS   7 am
       L'NC R'GT   7.5
       R Sc FUS   7.10
       {5th F.A. Bde (less 1 battery)}
           with amm cln   7.15
       57 Coy R.E (less 1 sect)   7.30
       4th Fd Amb.   7.40

3/ route   CHAMPROSE FM — CH la HOUSS-
                                      -AYE
4/ 30th Fd Artillery bde forms part of main
    body of left column of division.
    route LIVERDY — CHATRES and as in paral
    for left column. SP road junction
    point 105 just S of LIVERDY
       30th F.A. bde (less Amm Col)   6.15 am
       ditto   Amm col   6.35

5 Reports in right column to head of
                 main body

Issued by ...
at 11.15 pm
                              D Claus...
                              O/Bm 9th/18th

6.O.14/ 4

Operation Order No 25
by Brig. Gen. F.C.Shaw. C.B. Copy No
Cmdg Right Column

1/ The right flank of the enemy's advance appears to be a column of about 1 div. moving S.E. through LA FERTÉ — SOUS — JOUARRE.

The French forces to the N and E of us are taking the offensive.

The 3rd div advances in a NE direction tomorrow with 2nd div on right from FONTENAY on LUMIGNY and 5th div on left from TOURNAN on VILLENEUVE

The left clm of 3rd div via CH du CHEMIN - crossroads point 120 1 m. S of OBELISQUE

2/ Right Column. Order of march
 Adv. gd. Cmdr Lt. Col N.R. McMahon D.S.O 4/R.FUS

4/R.FUS
1 Sect 57 Coy. R.E.   } to rendezvous at road junction
1 batt 23rd Bde RFA   } ¼ m. N of CHATRES at 6 am

"A" Form.
MESSAGES AND SIGNALS.

Army Form C. 2121.

Prefix	Code	m.	Words	Charge	This message is on a/c of:	Recd. at	m.
Office of Origin and Service Instructions.			Sent			Date	
			At	m.	...............Service.	From	
			To				
			By		(Signature of "Franking Officer.")	By	

TO

Sender's Number	Day of Month	In reply to Number	A A A

4 Outposts will rejoin their Battalion by 4.30
am but will only leave their position as
late as possible to do so.

5 Report to head) of Wnkms

From
Place
Time

The above may be forwarded as now corrected. (Z)

Censor. Signature of Addresser or person authorised to telegraph in his name.

* This line should be erased if not required.

Mr. S. A. Andrée.

MESSAGES AND SIGNALS. Army Form C. 2121.

Prefix	Code	m.	Words	Charge	This message is on a/c of:	Recd. at ___ m.
Office of Origin and Service Instructions.			Sent			Date
			At ___ m.		___ Service.	From
			To			
			By		(Signature of "Franking Officer.")	By

TO Operation Orders No 8

Sender's Number: Brig Genl F C Shaw Cmdg 9th Inf Bde   Day of Month: 4   In reply to Number: AAA

Sept 4th

1. The enemy has crossed the R MARNE at several points E of MEAUX. The 3rd Division moves tonight.

2. Route CRECY — road junction ¼ mile S of BESSY CH — X roads ¼ m NW of B of BELLEVUE CH — OBELISKE — CH on CHEMIN CHARTRES..

3. Order of march
   Unit.   Starting pt.
                  MONTANSON FM
                  10.30 pm

From: 30th How Bde
      23rd FA Bde
      5?   70 Coy RE   Holtzmanig
Place: 30th How Bde
Time:

The above may be forwarded as now corrected.   (Z)

Censor.   Signature of Addressor or person authorised to telegraph in his name.
This line should be erased if not required.

"A" Form.   Army Form 2121.
MESSAGES AND SIGNALS.   No. of Message

TO: Operation Order No 24 Copy No 8
By Brig-Gen F.C. Shaw C.B.
Comdg 9th INF BDE

AAA

1. Our 1st Corps engaged enemy today about VILLERS COTTERETS 2nd and 5th Div. was about BETZ & NANTEUIL. The 4th Div engaged enemy rear and captured several guns about NERY

2. The 4 [illegible] FOSSE MARTIN — DOUY — MAROLLY — [illegible] — BARGNY — LA MARCHE — PEVY — [illegible] CHAUCONIN

3. Order of march

R.Sc Fus	Advd Guard	
30 Bde	3.30	}
57 Coy RE	3.40	} main body
23rd Bty	3.55	}
9th Fd Amb	4.15	}
No 2 Fd Coy	4.25	
From R Fus	4.30	
Place LNLR	4.15	

O.C. 8th Field Ambulances.

The Fld. Amb⁵ less three Ambulance Waggons each will move tonight to LESCHES via E of PENCHARD – first C of CHAUCONIN – TRILBARDOU bridge. AAA They will assemble with the head of the column at the E of PENCHARD at 6.30 p.m. and will march under orders of Lt Col. Stone 8th Fld Ambulance.

2 Sept 1914

A Chopping
Major R.A.M.C.

"C" Form (Original).
MESSAGES AND SIGNALS.
Army Form C. 2123.

TO: 9th Fd Amb.

Sender's Number.	Day of Month.	In reply to Number.	AAA
BM 17	First		

The troops in the 9th INF BDE area will be in fighting billets tonight. viz in a state of constant readiness to turn out at a moment's notice AAA The troops in the area are

9th INF BDE
30th (How) BDE R.F.A.
23rd BDE RFA
57 Coy RE
9th Fd Amb.

1/2/1

FROM: 9th INF BDE
PLACE: BOUILLANCY
TIME: 7.15 pm

"A" Form.
Army Form C.____

MESSAGES AND SIGNALS.

No. of Message____

Prefix____ Code____ m. | Words | Charge | This message is on ____ Ambulance ____ m.
Office of Origin and Service Instructions. | | | Annexe to ____ War Diary
____ | Sent | |
____ | At____ m. | | ____ From____
____ | To____ | | ____
____ | By____ | (Signature of "Franking Officer.") | By____ Coy N° 8

TO { Operation Orders N° 20

Sender's Number | Day of Month | In reply to Number | AAA
Brig Genl F C Shaw CB.
CRA 9th Infy Bde

VANCIENNES
Ref Sheets 33 . 49.   1st Sept.

1. Information has been circulated separately.

2. The 3rd Div marches to the area VILLERS – BREGY today

3. Troops in 9th Bde area march as follows the Heavy Battery following the 8th Infantry Bde Route VANCIENNES – LEVIGNEN – FRESNOY – VILLERS

From
Place
Time

The above may be forwarded as now corrected.   (Z)
Censor.   Signature of Addressor or person authorised to telegraph in his name.

WAR DIARY

INTELLIGENCE SUMMARY.
(Erase heading not required.)

Army Form C. 2118.

Instructions regarding War Diaries and Intelligence Summaries are contained in F.S. Regs., Part II. and the Staff Manual respectively. Title pages will be prepared in manuscript.

Hour, Date, Place	Summary of Events and Information	Remarks and references to Appendices
10 a.m. 22.9.14 VAILLY	On the afternoon of 21.9.14 received orders to proceed the same evening with the remainder of B Sectn. & transport of main Company & Pontoons left behind to VAILLY accompanied by HQ across the 16th C[ompany]. Intention to take over the Dressing Station there. Left BRAINE about 6-45 p.m. and reached VAILLY dressing station about 11 p.m. where we found the R.E. tents occupying their wounded. Left there LIEUT FLEMING (previously shell wound right leg) LIEUT J.O. HAMILTON (shrapnel of knee fatal wound) (who on died that night), also one female, four civilian Frenchmen & two wounded children. Cases arrived during the early hours of the morning and (22.9.14) plenty of stretcher bearers were sent out at the request of the Brigadier 16th Bde to bring in wounded. About 10-45 a.m. heavy shell fire started anew on to about 12.30 noon. The Church next door was struck in four places & by broken roof damaged & many of the windows of the dressing station were broken by fragments/concussion. We had to hurriedly evacuate the sick from the Church and only just in time when the full of masonry occurred, the one headed for cellar (found some under at the building) and filled over for sick and wounded into there and placed our lying down cases on the floor. When the firing ceased we cleared up the most sheltered part of the building and cleared the cellars and floated them out to a ready for casualties. About 4-30 p.m. the shelling started again and as far as possible everyone (not under cover, the firing lasted about 40 minutes about 6 pm. the cases were prepared for evacuation all had been evacuated to A & D Sectn. and A 36. were the wounded "all in". At 7 p.m. the front party all walking cases were started off under charge of an N.C.O. (32 wounded) (6 sick) walking cases was started off under charge officer, the stretcher cases followed immediately after the walking. LIEUT GOODING R.A.M.C. stayed in to oversee & LIEUT LETHBRIDGE took 2 men not shell early Left Knee) bleed included.	
10 a.m. 23.9.14 VAILLY		

Army Form C. 2118

WAR DIARY
INTELLIGENCE SUMMARY.
(Erase heading not required.)

Instructions regarding War Diaries and Intelligence Summaries are contained in F.S. Regs., Part II. and the Staff Manual respectively. Title pages will be prepared in manuscript.

Hour, Date, Place	Summary of Events and Information	Remarks and references to Appendices
10 a.m. 23.9.14 VAILLY	Two females wounded (from french ambulance and two children were also evacuated (all wounded). Captain HAWES LEICESTER Regmt Stretcher and 3 had penetrating shell and one I shrapnel in jaw. One was left and they were kept for removal. Also two private wounds of knee kept back on night of 21st operation order. At 12.30 a.m. morning of 23.9.14 CAPTAIN HAWES died having sprung on common. His effects were handed over by me to the Qr Mr 1st Btn 16th Bde personally. At the hour of writing there are only three cases in B section viz two fractured of head & one fractured of forearm. Staff Sergt LAMKIN R.A.M.C. went out under shell fire yesterday afternoon to bring in LIEUT. GOODING R.A.M.C. wounded by shell in this about.	
10-15 a.m. 24.9.14 VAILLY	Survey entered on a review of wounded struck much Revd C. Sexton was talking in." The shelling on the morning of the dressing station was heavy. Their the previous day, he wounded killed near. A large amount of ordnance equipment had collected two horses killed two wounded men. A portion their rifles, bayonets, webbing equipment, water bottles, canteens, etc. We were issued to replacements having a short trip. He remembers was by order of Ast Gen Sections away by an Officer R.S.C. in a cart at 7.30 a.m. The body of the late CAPTAIN HAWES LEICESTER REGMT was buried in the cemetery here and marked with a temporary Cross. About 7 p.m. evacuation was commenced, on cars, called to your head. Being sent from B Section" and 9 wounded lying down 3 walking cases from C Section. A quantity of laisine helpless in cycle form was received from BRAINE with verbal orders to send	Good

WAR DIARY
INTELLIGENCE SUMMARY.
(Erase heading not required.)

Army Form C. 2118.

Instructions regarding War Diaries and Intelligence Summaries are contained in F.S. Regs., Part II. and the Staff Manual respectively. Title pages will be prepared in manuscript.

Hour, Date, Place	Summary of Events and Information	Remarks and references to Appendices
10-15 am 24.9.14 VAILLY	Took men in the trenches. Spare clothes for 3 companies. HQ Coys of 8th & 18th Brigades informed after visits that they would make arrangements for the Regiment Commander to draw their supply from here. B section taking in from 6am today	
10-30 am 25.9.14 VAILLY	During the afternoon evening a few cases came in refractory and arrangement for wounded at 7 pm were ready. Nine officers and crews of Schreckli and 13 men chiefly wounded near the cut off output. On the cases were being despatched another officer & two men wounded here brought in & two w. officers disposed of by HA / received men were sent up the line with the artillery. At 7.30 pm orders were received from the 18th (3rd Division) to hand over the evening Station to two sections of no 16 F. Ambulance type. B/C action of no 9 F. Ambulance to return to BRAINE. The Equipment was packed & then left about 10 pm reaching BRAINE about 12-15 am on 25.9.14 at 10-15 am orders received to proceed to commence of B/C sects. no 9 F. Ambulance to COURCELLES about 3 kilometres E of BRAINE. To establish a dressing station there for 9th Brigade. Left at 12 noon and on reaching COURCELLES about 12.30 halted near the Q.C.; received instructions to encamp here & wait further orders on reaching a dressing station close field transp in the meanwhile.	
11-30 am 26.9.14 COURCELLES	Spent morning inspecting COURCELLES. Found in the centre of the village a fountain yielding especially good drinking water and a trap in the approach on the street selected area under the	Sgd.

WAR DIARY
of
INTELLIGENCE SUMMARY.
(Erase heading not required.)

Army Form C. 2118.

Instructions regarding War Diaries and Intelligence Summaries are contained in F.S. Regs., Part II. and the Staff Manual respectively. Title pages will be prepared in manuscript.

Hour, Date, Place	Summary of Events and Information	Remarks and references to Appendices
26.9.14 COURCELLES	The Corner of the Square Street was a Farm Yard with a pump giving water suitable for cooking purposes and all the wells visited for the men purposes in the WORN guarded. Up on arrival, water for horses was in a stream both the gutters through Caloucellus have been opened & Pte 1 N.S. Gordons are away to the sawmill where from the hill to ward farling of the period round the house had been long or during the day all equipment was cleaned. incident made not to complete. In the evening Franklin Routing inspection accompanied by Captain Fraser Russell were made approved Courlay — Upper ten minute., the men after detachment were housed in Barlow & Turk for night.	
12 noon. 27.9.14 COURCELLES	The Sanitary inspection made and visited the Bee House 20 by 60 was reported in the Brocard any condition. Of parts of the village Send the following recommendations	
(a) Water supply. That the Fountain & top supply in the Courlay gardens should be used for drinking under sentries portal in them to ensure enough that the other two supplies should be used for cooking and to water also two sections pails and that the supplies which are temporarily by Captain Fraser Russell (Sanitary officer) should be close to the here for the present.		
The stream of S.a. gueleus both used for horses & the kitchen Grove down to washing clothing of men.		

WAR DIARY
INTELLIGENCE SUMMARY.
(Erase heading not required.)

Army Form C. 2118.

Instructions regarding War Diaries and Intelligence Summaries are contained in F.S. Regs., Part II. and the Staff Manual respectively. Title pages will be prepared in manuscript.

Hour, Date, Place	Summary of Events and Information	Remarks and references to Appendices
27.9.14. COURCELLES	(B) Latrines. Had about latrines to atrine urinals in the gardens behind the houses cleanly by the men. Also arm pits and that burnt lime to be provided when possible for arm pits to be emptied in the mornings into the urinal pits. (C) Had fatigues parties with candles out to employ the many manure yards and other places in the billeting area which are now in a very filthy condition.	
28.9.14 COURCELLES 12 noon	During the early part of the morning accompanied by the Secretary of the Mayor made an inspection of the area occupied. Found that a good deal of refuse had been standing up. The broken supplies drain sewers &c and that scavengers had been posted in sufficient. He would at the S.W. of the village which is a very dirty place. Also unused waste land being used in places infected and are being kept in a pretty untidy/insanitary condition. The streets and billets were much cleaner and more kept up to appearance than been made to improve matters. Found two carts to the N.E. of the village and the mill for sanitary orders have a scheme for the purchase of slacked manure, and was selected for filling out under carts, for emptying manure in the care if cant when the following arrangements and order, arrangements made with the Gov. for new oubry pre to prevent contamination of the supply. Attention was also drawn to the common places where the General had	

Army Form C. 2118

WAR DIARY
or
INTELLIGENCE SUMMARY
(Erase heading not required.)

Instructions regarding War Diaries and Intelligence Summaries are contained in F.S. Regs., Part II. and the Staff Manual respectively. Title pages will be prepared in manuscript.

Hour, Date, Place	Summary of Events and Information	Remarks and references to Appendices
12 noon 28.9.14 COURCELLES	Been fouled.	
5-30 pm 29.9.14 COURCELLES	Made a sanitary inspection with Sanitary Officer and found a marked improvement. The water supply arrangements seem to be working satisfactorily. The village is much cleaner and the latrines in use appear to be receiving attention. The hospital & 3 officers wards, the dressing stations and ceased dressings that the battle cases were not in use and intended plans for any extensive emergency were being discussed. No steps being transferred to the clearing hospital cases were delirious. Except on urgent medical grounds or grave complications that uncertainly some families BRAISNE. I had thought it would be wiser to evacuate every equipment to places of very short notice. The necessary special case would be cleared and mattress cases filled after the uses the dressing station was cleared and mattress cases filled.	
1 pm 30.9.14 COURCELLES	Sanitary inspection made & various suggestions arrived. A Kitch up and f Adv H Gr. 8th Bde. showing areas that required further cleaning up. A parade of all stretcher bearers of the [und] ambulance ran on duty here at 12 noon. Orders received from O.C. 9 F. Amb. to send our teams and drivers with its waggons to the Cr. no. 9 F. Amb. of Sharon to assist in evacuation from VAILLY.	

9th Field Ambulance

Vol III

1/11/1917
22/12/1914
S/1

WAR DIARY
INTELLIGENCE SUMMARY.
(Erase heading not required.)

Army Form C. 2118.

Instructions regarding War Diaries and Intelligence Summaries are contained in F.S. Regs., Part II. and the Staff Manual respectively. Title pages will be prepared in manuscript.

Hour, Date, Place	Summary of Events and Information	Remarks and references to Appendices
11 p.m. 1-10-14. BRAINE.	Received order (attached) from A.D.M.S. to bring in "B" & "C" sections, prepare for move, and await further orders. This was done.	(order attached 1.)
11 p.m. 2-10-14. CRAMAILLE.	Received orders to march at 5 p.m. to AUGY. On the march received orders to follow the second of the two battalions at AUGY to SERVENAY, after joining the column, destination was changed to CRAMAILLE where unit has gone into billets.	(order attached 2.)
6 p.m. 3-10-14. CRAMAILLE.	Have just received order to march by BEUGNEUX – LE PLESSIER HULEU – BILLY SUROURCQ – CHOUY – NOROY to TROESNES; unit to have starting point (CRAMOISELLE), at 6:50 p.m. Under order from D.A.D.M.S. 3rd Division have just sent 2 ambulance wagons to GRAND ROZOY under Lieut. TULLOCH to march with Worcester Regt.	(order attached 3.)
6 p.m. 4-10-14. TROESNES.	Marched according to orders. Received order to march to CREPY EN VALOIS. Starting point of Lieut. SILLY Railway Station at 6-5-5 p.m. Lieut. TULLOCH with 2 ambulance wagons rejoined at COYOLLIES.	(orders attached 4.)
6 p.m. 5-10-14. CREPY.	Marched according to orders. Received orders to march tonight to area RHUIS–MORU–ROBERVAL, by route DUVY–RULLY–VILLENEUVE. Starting point	(orders attached 5.)

Army Form C. 2118.

WAR DIARY
or
INTELLIGENCE SUMMARY.
(Erase heading not required.)

Instructions regarding War Diaries and Intelligence Summaries are contained in F. S. Regs., Part II. and the Staff Manual respectively. Title pages will be prepared in manuscript.

Hour, Date, Place	Summary of Events and Information	Remarks and references to Appendices
5-10-14. Continued	Unit of unit CREPY Railway Station at 4 p.m. Have cleared sick collected on night marches to clearing hospital established at Railway Station.	GNK
10 a.m. 6-10-14. ROBERVAL.	Marched according to orders received when near ROBERVAL where unit is billetted; attached orders for entrainment at LE MEUX, to arrive there at 2 p.m. today and depart at 6 p.m.	(Order attached 6) GNK
8.30 a.m. 7-10-14. ABBEVILLE	Arrived here about 11 a.m., have detrained and received order to march to GRAND LAVIERS, unit clearing sick (including Sgt Major of Unit) to French Military Hospital in the town, by instruction of P.A.D.M.S. Stayed on road at GRAND LAVIERS during most of the day, and, in the afternoon received order to proceed to the village where went in to billets.	(Order attached 7) GNK
11 p.m. 7-10-14. PORT-LE-GRAND.		GNK
11 p.m. 8.10.14. PORT LE GRAND.	Have received orders to march by LE PLESSIEL-CANCHY LE BOISLE to TOLLENT, starting point crossroads just S.E. of BUIGNY at 2.45 p.m. tonight.	(Order attached 8) GNK
5 p.m. 9-10-14. TOLLENT.	Marched last night according to orders and reached here soon after 8 a.m. and have just received orders attached. Dismounted men (under Major BLISS with Lieuts	GNK

WAR DIARY
INTELLIGENCE SUMMARY.
(Erase heading not required.)

Army Form C. 2118.

Hour, Date, Place	Summary of Events and Information	Remarks and references to Appendices
9-10-14 (Continued)	Lieuts TULLOCH and CARBERRY) to march behind remainder of unit to REGNAUVILLE there to await transport by motor. Mounted portion of unit with horses and vehicles to march in column under command of Lt Col. BUTLER, R.F.A. to TANGRY. O.C. unit with remainder of officers marches with this party.	(order attached 9)
12 noon, 10-10-14. TANGRY.	Arrived here after long march about 11 a.m. Various occupied much increased by checks in column in front, chiefly due to hills and bad surface roads. Marches by CAUMONT — REGNAUVILLE — GUIGNY — ST. GEORGE — BERMICOURT — FLEURY — HESTRUS. Found on arrival dismounted party at TANGRY.	(order attached 10)
11 p.m. 11-10-14. L'ECLEME.	Received orders to move to HAUTRIEUX; marched on to first outside ROBECQ; received in late afternoon orders to return here to billet.	(order attached 11)

WAR DIARY
INTELLIGENCE SUMMARY.
(Erase heading not required.)

Army Form C. 2118.

Instructions regarding War Diaries and Intelligence Summaries are contained in F.S. Regs., Part II. and the Staff Manual respectively. Title pages will be prepared in manuscript.

Hour, Date, Place	Summary of Events and Information	Remarks and references to Appendices
11 am 12/14 CROSS ROADS ½ m E of LE CORNET MALO	Orders attached received. Sent out bearer Sub-divisions to keep in touch with infantry battalions; all transport remained in billets till divisional order (attached) received to move on. Orders received to send officer with a requisitioning country cart to form part of brigade column to draw Ordnance Stores here, CARBERRY detailed for this duty. Marched by BASSEE – PT. LEVIS – LE CORNET MALO with the objective LA CROIX MARMUSE. Have however found it un-Inable to pass this point on account of blocking of roads chiefly by the French. Have parked in a field; wounded are being collected.	(Order attached[?]) [signature]
11 pm 13/14 ZELOBES.	Left Major HUDLESTON with tent subdivisions of C. Section, and wounded and moved on to a point about ½ mile west of ZELOBES; wounded collected here during the day. Major HUDLESTON rejoined with his party and unit moved into billets under verbal divisional order at ZELOBES where a dressing station has been formed. Large numbers of wounded are being collected.	[signature]

WAR DIARY
INTELLIGENCE SUMMARY
(Erase heading not required.)

Army Form C. 2118.

Instructions regarding War Diaries and Intelligence Summaries are contained in F. S. Regs., Part II. and the Staff Manual respectively. Title pages will be prepared in manuscript.

Hour, Date, Place	Summary of Events and Information	Remarks and references to Appendices
11 p.m. 14/11. ZELOBES.	Unit cleared of wounded today, by motor convoy. Chief points of collection for this unit are FOSSE, VIEILLE CHAPELLE and LA COUTURE, again large numbers of wounded being collected, further clearance by night Convoy. Lt TULLOCH and ELKINGTON with 2 NCOs and 19 men left for BETHUNE under orders of D.D.M.S. 2nd A. Corps.	[signature]
11 p.m. 15/11. ZELOBES.	The clearance of the unit by motor convoy was done last night by relays of cars through the night and was most satisfactory. Again large numbers of wounded are being collected.	[signature]
11 p.m. 16/11. FARMHOUSES ½ mile N of X ROADS at C of CROIX BARBÉE.	Left Major HUDLESTON with "C" tent subdivision and in accordance with order attached sent out personnel of a tent subdivision (to keep in touch with battalions of 9th Infy Bde) and moved remainder of unit into VIEILLE CHAPELLE. Invited here for several hours during which D.A.D.M.S. visited unit and stated that it would now work under divisional orders only. Ordered (verbally) on to billet at X roads N of C in CROIX BARBÉE. Have gone into billets here in nearest buildings. A few wounded are being collected. O.C. unit proceeded to	(Order attached no. 13) [signature]

WAR DIARY
INTELLIGENCE SUMMARY
(Erase heading not required.)

Army Form C. 2118.

Hour, Date, Place	Summary of Events and Information	Remarks and references to Appendices
11 pm 16/10/14 (Continued)	to 9th Inf Bde H'Qrs at ROUGE CROIX to keep touch and returned with information but no orders. Ambulance collecting a few wounded. 2 Battalions of Bedfs at FAUQUISSART and two at CHAPIGNY.	Smith
11 pm 17/10/14 ROUGE CROIX.	Under divisional orders (verbal), moved about noon to ROUGE CROIX for billets and prepared a dressing station. Personally to this had sent forward stretcher subdivisions and ambulance wagons to keep touch with advancing Brigade. Capt B. ROBERTS and HABGOOD with bearers, Ambulance wagon party under Capt FRASER also sent forward. Capt ROBERTS' party reached AUBERS, a house was chosen as a dressing station near church. Towards evening C.O. of unit brought forward ambulance wagons. "A" Section forage cart and personnel of "A" sent Subdivision to AUBERS and dressing station was formed. About 100 wounded are being collected there.	(Order attached No 4) Smith
11.30 pm 18/10/14 ROUGE CROIX.	Motor ambulance lorry cleared dressing station at AUBERS and ROUGE CROIX this morning. Heavy fighting	Smith

Army Form C. 2118.

WAR DIARY
INTELLIGENCE SUMMARY.
(Erase heading not required.)

Instructions regarding War Diaries and Intelligence Summaries are contained in F. S. Regs., Part II. and the Staff Manual respectively. Title pages will be prepared in manuscript.

Hour, Date, Place	Summary of Events and Information	Remarks and references to Appendices
11.50 pm 18/10 (Continued)	fighting. Have evacuated AUBERS dressing station on account of being shelled this; re-established at another in LES MOILLES farm outside town. To this point Major HUDLESTON, with additional tent sub-division personnel has proceeded. Many wounded are being collected, in estimated total number 200. Motor convoy commenced clearing LES MOILLES farm dressing station about noon. Lieut. CARBERY rejoined. Evening clearance by ambulance wagons from HERLIES, LA CLIQUETERIE and AUBERS.	Gen'l
11 p.m. 19/10 ROUGE CROIX.	Collected wounded and cleared by motor convoy this morning.	Gen'l
11 p.m. 20/10 ROUGE CROIX.	Collected wounded from AUBERS, BUSCH farm and L'IVENTURE (firing line having been reinforced) cleared by motor convoy this morning.	Gen'l
11 p.m. 21/10 ROUGE CROIX	At 2 a.m. this morning the whole of advanced dressing station detachment returned to ROUGE CROIX, under advice from 9th Brigade Head Quarters bringing wounded.	Gen'l
11 p.m. 22/10 ROUGE CROIX		Gen'l

Army Form C. 2118.

WAR DIARY
INTELLIGENCE SUMMARY.
(Erase heading not required.)

Instructions regarding War Diaries and Intelligence Summaries are contained in F.S. Regs., Part II. and the Staff Manual respectively. Title pages will be prepared in manuscript.

Hour, Date, Place	Summary of Events and Information	Remarks and references to Appendices
22/7/14 (Continued)	wounded. At 11 a.m. motor convoy cleared. At 6 p.m. wagons and limbers under Capts ROBERTS and HABGOOD cleared wounded from PIETRE, AUBERS and BAS POMMEREAU. At 8 a.m. divisional recce ordered return to road junction, point ½ mile north of CROIX BARBEE.	G.H.L.
11 p.m. 23/7/14 VIEILLE CHAPELLE	Move mentioned in last note completed by 1 a.m. At 9 a.m. cleared by motor convoy. Moved under divisional order to VIEILLE CHAPELLE - FOSSE road; buildings on VIEILLE CHAPELLE - FOSSE road, near cross roads allotted	G.H.L.
11 p.m. 24/7/14 VIEILLE CHAPELLE	wounded from line of CHAPIGNY - NEUVE CHAPELLE Road. Cleared by motor convoy, collected from area last mentioned.	G.H.L.
11 p.m. 25/7/14 VIEILLE CHAPELLE	Cleared by motor Convoy; collecting tonight from area last mentioned. About 60 cronulates and separates, all limbers and wagons out.	G.H.L.
6 a.m. 26/7/14 VIEILLE CHAPELLE	Two journeys of collecting parties last night. Cleared this morning by motor convoy.	G.H.L.

Army Form C. 2118.

WAR DIARY
INTELLIGENCE SUMMARY.
(Erase heading not required.)

Instructions regarding War Diaries and Intelligence Summaries are contained in F. S. Regs., Part II. and the Staff Manual respectively. Title pages will be prepared in manuscript.

Hour, Date, Place	Summary of Events and Information	Remarks and references to Appendices
6.30am & 10.45am 26/9/14 NEILLE CHAPELLE	Received verbal orders to assume command of No 9 Field Ambulance. Lt.Col McLOUGHLIN having been appointed A.D.M.S. 3rd Division, from Colonel PORTER. A.M.S. D.M.S. Lt. Colonel McLOUGHLIN handed over and left about mid-day. Sent Capt FRASER to choose a suitable building for advanced dressing station and interior of Brigade Staff as to suitability, he reported that he had arranged with the Staff for occupation of farm buildings about 200 yards E of road junction 1/2 M west of the C in CROIX BARBEE. Informed Staff of establishment of Dressing Station.	
2.30pm	Capt FRASER 2 nursing orderlies & Runner, 1 Sergt, 1 Amb; wagon, 1 forage cart proceeded there, the arrangement being in reliefs of 24 hours. The remaining ambulance wagons with Capt ROBERTS and Lieut. DARBERY dispatched at 5.45pm with bearer sub divisions of 2 sections; wounded began to come in about 9pm, and from then onwards till 5.30 am.	

EWKhles
Major RAMC

WAR DIARY
INTELLIGENCE SUMMARY.
(Erase heading not required.)

Army Form C. 2118.

Hour, Date, Place	Summary of Events and Information	Remarks and references to Appendices
6 pm 24/10/1914. ZELOBES.	Some 115 men admitted including 4 officers. Many cases were very severe rifle shot wounds at close quarters showing marked explosive effect. Major HUDLESTON and I did the work at the Dressing Station assisted during the early hours of morning by Capt HABGOOD. At 4 a.m. notified ADMS by message that probable number of wounded for evacuation 130 to 140. The unit is much too short of officers (3) and the work falls heavily on those left. The Chaplain Revd ROWAN rendered most valuable services last night in going off with parties of bearers collecting the wounded from the Regimental Stretcher Bearers all being under fire at times (coming over trenches apparently). At 12.30 pm. orders from ADMS 3rd Divt. to move unit at once to ZELOBES and take over buildings, sent Capt ROBERTS on to try and get trams we had previously seen dressing Station, but before starting Red Cross Motor Ambulance Wagons arrived.	I

E W Ahier

WAR DIARY
INTELLIGENCE SUMMARY.
(Erase heading not required.)

Army Form C. 2118.

Hour, Date, Place	Summary of Events and Information	Remarks and references to Appendices
27-10-14 (Continued)	arrived and evacuated all lying down cases left. The walking cases were sent on by 1 N.C.O. Other walking wagons arrived and went after the walking caravan picked them up. Unit moved off about 1.15 p.m. and went to its billets at ZELOBES. Dressing station was opened by "B" Section. "C" Section standing by ready to go and form advanced dressing station if available spot was indicated by 9th Brigade to whom message asking for information had been sent.	
6 p.m. 28th/14 ZELOBES.	About 11.30 a.m. 32 cases were sent back from the Advanced Dressing Station at BOUT DEVILLE. There were two German wounded amongst them, one an officer. G.S., 2nd Division notified this. Papers collected ready for handing over. The cases were rather severe a number of cases of compound fracture of thigh &c. being amongst them, all were dressed and splinted and evacuated between 8 and 10.30 by Red Cross motor ambulance wagons. Numbers of wounded notified.	EWA

WAR DIARY

INTELLIGENCE SUMMARY.
(Erase heading not required.)

Hour, Date, Place	Summary of Events and Information	Remarks and references to Appendices
28/10/14 (continued)	ratified to A.D.M.S. 3rd Divn, and information given to Red Cross Convoy that the cases probably arrive 80 would require evacuation from advanced Dressing Station. Information that some ordnance stores were at a point 4 miles W of BETHUNE road. One ambulance wagon and N.C.O. sent to collect same. Shortage of officers much felt at Dressing Station, nobody to give anesthetics. 1 rich evacuated with the wounded. Cpl Chamberlain, Dysentery & Cpl Crowe both of R amb sent down to Clearing H BETHUNE. This brings the shortage of Personnel to about 40. A.D.M.S. came to enquire number for evacuation and stores taken. Obtained from him 50 blankets and dressings. Asked for at least 1 officer to carry on. Red Cross Convoy. 5 cars arrived about 12.30 midnight directed on to advanced Dressing Station, no wounded having been	
6 p.m. 29/10/14 ZELOBES.	arrived here from a Dressing Station, all having been	

WAR DIARY
INTELLIGENCE SUMMARY.
(Erase heading not required.)

Army Form C. 2118.

Hour, Date, Place	Summary of Events and Information	Remarks and references to Appendices
29/10/14 (Continued)	been evacuated direct. Officer i/c Motor Convoy arrived about 9 a.m. and took on four motor ambulance waggons to Advanced Dressing Station to be used during the day for evacuation. Major HUDLESTON reported two cabulets for 24 hrs about 60; surgical stores sent up to him at noon. Informed him return of casualties should be in early enough to enable me to render it by 6 a.m. daily. Saw Major EVANS, R.A.M.C. i/c motor ambulance transport and pointed out advantage of leaving a few cars at disposal by 10 p.m. nightly to collect lightly wounded cases from Advanced Dressing Station. Temporary Lieut. J.S. WILSON arrived from BETHUNE 20:6 Clearing Hosp. for duty. Very heavy firing at night but not casualties not in proportion. 7 a.m. went up to BOUT DE VILLE to see how matters were at Advanced Dressing Station. 6 cases there and things found to be satisfactory. One	
6 p.m. 30/10/14 ZELOBES.		

WAR DIARY

INTELLIGENCE SUMMARY.
(Erase heading not required.)

Army Form C. 2118.

Hour, Date, Place	Summary of Events and Information	Remarks and references to Appendices
30/10/14 (continued)	One wounded man admitted to main dressing station 2-2.30pm. Surgeon Genl. McPherson came to inspect the Dressing Station, called his attention to the shortage of stretchers and blankets & difficulty in getting them returned from clearing hospital; also saw Col. PORTER. D.D.M.S. and called his attention to the same matter. Orders received from 9th Brigade to march at once via LESTREM - LAGORGUE to ESTAIRES, moved off at 3 pm. having sent Lieut. CARBERY as billeting officer and notified O.C. Seaforths to join me at LESTREM with all leaders, het this portion of the unit on N side of LESTRUM and arrived at billets at 7pm. Men billeted in barns. Officers in two rooms in cottage. 9pm. received orders to march at 9am. the next morning in rear of 5th. Lancers to NEUVE EGLISE.	

WAR DIARY
INTELLIGENCE SUMMARY
(Erase heading not required.)

Army Form C. 2118.

Hour, Date, Place	Summary of Events and Information	Remarks and references to Appendices
10 p.m. 31/10 About 1 m. N. of BRANOUTRE	5.30 am orders from 9th Bde 3rd Div to march at 7 am in rear of transport of Lincolns and 5th Fusiliers to NEUVE EGLISE. Arrived there 10.30 am having crossed the BELGIAN Frontier at a point about 2½ Kilometres N.W. of STEENWERCK. On arrival at NEUVE EGLISE orders to park in a field there and await orders. About 10.30 am orders to march on independently to BRANOUTRE which we did arriving there about 12 noon. Halted awaiting orders. Unable to find any staff officer or get any orders. Place full of transport of 2nd and 3rd Cavalry Brigades. About 1 p.m. saw requisitioning officer 9th Brigade and arranged with him to take my unit on and billet at LOCRE or at one of the farms on the LOCRE – BRANOUTRE road and to inform R.S.O. of our position. Proceeded to farm in right of this road about 1½ kilometres N of BRANOUTRE. Cycle orderly sent to H.Q. 8-3 pm ordering me to remain at billets after 6.30 am following morning, ready to move off at short notice.	E.W.B. End of October 1914. E.W.Ellis Raynham O.C. 2nd Siege 5 Bat.

O.C.
9th Field

2 Btn 9th Inf Bde move to
AUGY tonight. AAA
No 9 Field Ambulance to
establish connection with
these, and move with the
9th /Bde.

↓
tomorrow

Braisne.
1-10-14.

A Cropping
Major RAMC
DADMS

3rd Division

I have allotted 9th Field
Ambulance to 9th Infty Bde
today. O.C. 9th Field Ambulance
he has requested orders from
9th Inf Bde. he has referred
him to 3rd Division. Shall
I move him to AUGY where
2 Battns of 9th Bde are, if so
if there any objection to the
unit moving there by day
light. _____ 5

Move 9th F. Amb: at 5.30 p.m.
as the whole Bde Hqrs in Augy are
moving again at A Cuthbury
6 p.m. Major name
R Roy Lt Col D A D M S
BRAISNE
2—10—14 3rd Division
12.10 P.M.

"A" Form.   Army Form C. 2121.

MESSAGES AND SIGNALS.

TO: 9th & Fd: Amb.

Sender's Number: A 1067
Day of Month: 2nd
AAA

The 9th Fd Amb will follow the 2 Battalions of the 9th Inf Bde which leave AUGY at 6pm and will march with them to billets at SERVENAY.

From: 2nd Div
Time: 5. 2pm

Prefix	Code
Office of Origin and Service Instructions	

Sent
At ____ m.
To ____
By ____

This message is on a/c of:
____ Service.
(Signature of "Franking Officer.") ③

Recd. at ____ m.
Date ____
From ____
By ____

TO O.C. 9th Field Ambulance

Sender's Number	Day of Month	In reply to Number	
M 216	3-10-14		AAA

Sent two Ambulance Waggons at once to join the Worcester Regiment at GRAND ROZOY and march with them. AAA. The two waggons should remain at COYOLLES and join you tomorrow as your Field Ambulance passes through COYOLLES.

From: Medical
Place: 3rd Division
Time:

The above may be forwarded as now corrected.
(Z)
Censor. Signature of Addressee or person authorised to telegraph in his name

A Godfrey Major
D.A.D.M.S.

Operation Order No 3
by
Adam- Brig Genl F C Shaw C.B.

(4)

SILLY
4-10-14.

1. The 9 Bde Group will march to CREPY EN VALOIS tonight in accordance with attached march table. Transport A & B will accompany units.

2. Route will be issued to O.C units later

3. Reports to head of Main Body

J M Paueter Capt
B M. 9 Inf Bde

4-10-14.

Unit	Starting Point	Trains
Bde H⁰qrs	Road Junct PT PORT	6.5 pm
Linc R	SILLY RY Station	5-6.55 pm
R. Scs Fus	Billets	6.10 pm
North'd Fus	Road Junct PT PORT	6.15 pm
R. Fus	SILLY RY Station	6.15 pm
23 FA Bde (less Amm Col)	"	6.20 pm
57 Fd Coy RE	Road Junct PT PORT	6.50 pm
Amm Col	SILLY RY Station	6.40 pm
F'd Amb	"	6.55 pm
Train		7 pm

Operation Order No 4
by
Brig General Shaw CB Commdg 9 Inf Bde

Ref SOISSONS & BEAUVAIS maps.

CREPY
5-10-14

(1) The 9th Bde group will march to the area RHUIS – MORU – ROBERVAL tonight in accordance with attached march table.

(2) Route DUVY – RULLY – VILLENEUVE

(3) Reports to head of main body

J M Tolletin Capt
BM 9th Inf Bde

March Table

Units	Starting Point	Time
Bde Hd Qrs	←Open place at CREPY Station→	6.4 p.m.
R. Sco Fus		6.5 p.m.
Northd Fus		6.10 p.m.
R. Fus		6.15 p.m.
Line Regt		6.20 p.m.
23 F.A. Bde		6.25 p.m.
(less Amm Col)		
5.7 Fd Coy R.E.		6.40 p.m.
Amm Col		6.45 p.m.
9 Fd Amb		7 p.m.
Train		7.10 p.m.

ORDERS — G.O.C. 9ᵗʰ Bde Area.

11 Amd.

1. Units will entrain as under. An officer will be sent by each unit to reconnoitre the entraining station previous to the time of arrival of the unit.

Train no.	Unit	Station	Time of arrival at Station	Time of Departure
19	Linc. R, 1 sect RE	LE MEUX	6 a.m.	10 a.m.
21	R. Scots. Fus. Bde Hd Qrs	PONT ST. MAXENCE	8 a.m.	12 noon
22	R. Fus. 1 sect RE	LONGUEIL	9 a.m.	1 p.m.
25	North'd Fus, 1 sect RE	PONT ST. MAXENCE	12 noon	4 p.m.
27	Fd. Amb. remainder RE	LE MEUX	2 p.m.	6 p.m.
28	29 Coy A.S.C.	COMPEIGNE	3 p.m.	7 p.m.
29	1 Bty 23 F.A. Bde. 1 sect. AMN. Col.	PT. ST. MAXENCE	4 p.m.	8 p.m.
30	1 Bty 23 F.A. Bde. 1 sect. AMN Col.	LONGUEIL	5 p.m.	9 p.m.
31	1 Bty 23 F.A. Bde. 1 sect. Amn. Col.	LE MEUX	6 p.m.	10 p.m.
33	Extra train for units not accommodated	PONT ST. MAXENCE	8 p.m.	12 m.n.

2. O.C. 57" Field Coy will arrange to divide his unit into 3 sections & will inform O.C. units with whom these sections entrain of their strength & composition.

3. O.C. 23rd F.A. Bde. will arrange for the entrainment & division into 3 sections of the AMN. COL.

4. Parts of units for which no accommodation can be found will proceed by train no. 33. The R.T.O. being previously informed.

5. Units will entrain complete with Baggage & Supply wagons.

issued on arrival of Bde. in billeting area.

J. Harold
Lieut
Staff Capt.
9th Inf. Bde.

Ask D.A.Q.M.G.
for orders for No 9
Field Ambulance

Hotel de Boeuf.

Billeting Officer now arranging for
billets in No. 9 Brigade area. Please
move to ~~Grand~~ GRAND
LAVIERS about 2 miles N.W
of ABBEVILLE, & await
billeting officers instructions.

C. N. Maynard, Major
D.A.A.Q.M.G.

Hotel de Boeuf
8. a. m.

⑧

Operation Order No 6
by
Brig. General F.C. Shaw C.B.
Comdg. 9th Infy. Bde.

Ref. maps 11, 12 & 7.

BUIGNY
8-10-14

1. The 9th Bde group will march tonight in accordance with attached march table. Transports A & B will accompany units.

2. Route – LE PLESSIEL – CANCHY – LE BOISLE to billets about TOLLENT

3. North'd Fusiliers & R. Fus. will each detail one officer & two N.C.O.s & Linc. R & R. Sc. Fus. two N.C.O.s each to march just in front of Field Ambulance & bring on Stragglers. They will join the Fd. Ambce. at the starting point

4. Reports to Head of Column

Issued at 3 p.m.

J.M. Crichton Captain
Bde. Maj. 9. Infy. Bde.

MARCH TABLE

Starting Point

Unit	Time
Bde H.Q.[?]	1.45 a.m.
North'd Fus	1.50
R. Fus	1.55
Line R	2.0
R. Bc. Fus	2.5
23. F.A Bde	2.10
(less am. Col)	
57. 9.D Coy R.E.	2.25
Am. Col.	2.30
9. F. Ambce	2.45
Train	2.50

Cross Rds just S.E of BUICNY

The Line R will reach the road by then, will clear until North'd Fus & R. Fus have passed.

The train will not come on to the road until the Ammunition Column has passed.

Operation Order No. 7.
by
Brig. Genl. F.C. Shaw. C.B.
Comdg. 9° Infy. Bde

Reference Map No. 7.   TOLLENT   9.10.14

1. The 1st Line Transport including officers chargers & bicycles (less blanket wagons) & the baggage & supply section will move at 6.45 p.m. as follows.

Officer in charge Maj. T.P. Wallock, DSO 4/R. Fus.
Starting Point CAUMONT CHURCH
Order of March - Line R
                  North. Fus
                  R. Fus.
                  R. Sc. Fus
                  ~~22 Fd. Amb~~
                  ~~57 ~~~~ R.E.~~
                  ~~5~~ ~~Fd Ambce~~

It will arrive at the Road junction just W of EREMBEAUCOURT at 8 p.m. with the head clear of the main road, marching via CHERIENNE. It will then come under the orders of O.C. Divl. Train and march to TANGRY.

(2) The Bde less all horses & vehicles except blanket wagons will march in accordance with attached march table via REGNAUVILLE — HESDIN to X roads just S. of AVOHY. The dismounted portions of mounted units will join the rear of the column at REGNAUVILLE.

(A Cont'd)

3. On arrival at REGNAUVILLE the whole will move by motor lorries to PERNES.

4. Reports to head of column.

                    J.M. ????? Captain
                    Bde. Maj. 9° Infy Bde.

"A" Form. Army Form C. 2121.
MESSAGES AND SIGNALS.

TO: 9th Bde

Sender's Number	Day of Month	In reply to Number	AAA
BM 81	9		

Reference Operation Order No 3 for REGNAUVILLE read X roads 3 of AUCHY

From: 9 Bde
Time: 6-15 pm

9, F^d-Arnde

"A" Form. Army Form 2121
MESSAGES AND SIGNALS.   No. of Message

Prefix	Code		Words	Charge	This message is on a/c of:	Recd. at .... m.
Office of Origin and Service Instructions.			Sent			Date
			At .... m.			From
			To			
			By		(Signature of "Franking Officer.")	By

TO   9th Fd Ambulance

Sender's Number	Day of Month	In reply to Number	A A A
*GA 89	Tenth		

Dwn will be ready to move as follows aaa 8th Infy bde 7.0am 7th Infy bde 8.0am starting pt eastern exit of PERNES aaa 9th bde 7.0am starting pt eastern exit of SICHIN Dwn mtd troops 6.30am 56th and 57th Coy RE 7.0am Compo Coy RE 6.0am 46th FA bde 6.0am 23rd and 42nd FA bdes 7.0am 30th hours and heavy batty 8.0am Operation orders will follow later. aaa A Bearer sub dw of each field ambulance will be ready to accompany each infy bde Operation orders will be issued 5.0am 3rd Dw

From
Place
Time   9.20 pm

The above may be forwarded as now corrected.   (Z)
                                                 Censor.   Signature of Addressor or person authorised to telegraph in his name.
* This line should be erased if not required.

O.C.
   9th Field Ambulance.

Please bring your Field Ambulance
to Cross Roads LA C'tx MARMUSE
Route along the Canal Road
passed BASSEE — P'te LEVIS —
LE CORNET MALO LA C'tx
MARMUSE.

LA TOMBE WILLOT.   A Cumming
   12.55 P.M   Major RAMC
   12-10-14   DADMS

"A" Form.
MESSAGES AND SIGNALS.
Army Form C. 2121.
No. of Message _____

Prefix ___ Code ___ m.	Words	Charge	This message is on a/c of:	Recd. at ___ m.
Office of Origin and Service Instructions.	Sent At ___ m. To ___ By ___		___ Service. (Signature of "Franking Officer.")	Date From ⑬ By

TO 9ᵗʰ Field Ambulance

Sender's Number	Day of Month	In reply to Number	AAA
SC 216	16		

The Brigade is established between PM 17 and Rouge Croix on the ESTAIRES — NEUVE CHAPELLE Road send the Personnel of a Bearer Sub Div at 7 a.m. to Transport "B" of the Brigade and move into VIEILLE CHAPELLE yourself AAA Bde HQ & TPT "B" are at X Road Due N of 1ᵂ E in CHAPELLE we intend moving on at 7.30 am in an Easterly Direction

From Place 9ᵗʰ INF BDE
Time

The above may be forwarded as now corrected. (Z) ___ Censor. Signature of Addresser or person authorised to telegraph in his name.

* This line should be erased if not required.

"A" Form.

MESSAGES AND SIGNALS

Prefix	Code	Words	Charge				
Office of Origin and Service Instructions		Sent At m. To By		This message is o... (Signature of "Franking Officer.")		...ed. at m. Date From By	

TO — 9th Amb.   (14)

Sender's Number	Day of Month	In reply to Number	AAA
BM 211	16		

Please send the whole of the bearer personnel of your bearer sub-division up to Bde. Hd. Qrs.

From   9 Bde
Place
Time   7-55 am

The above may be forwarded as now corrected.   (Z)

BM

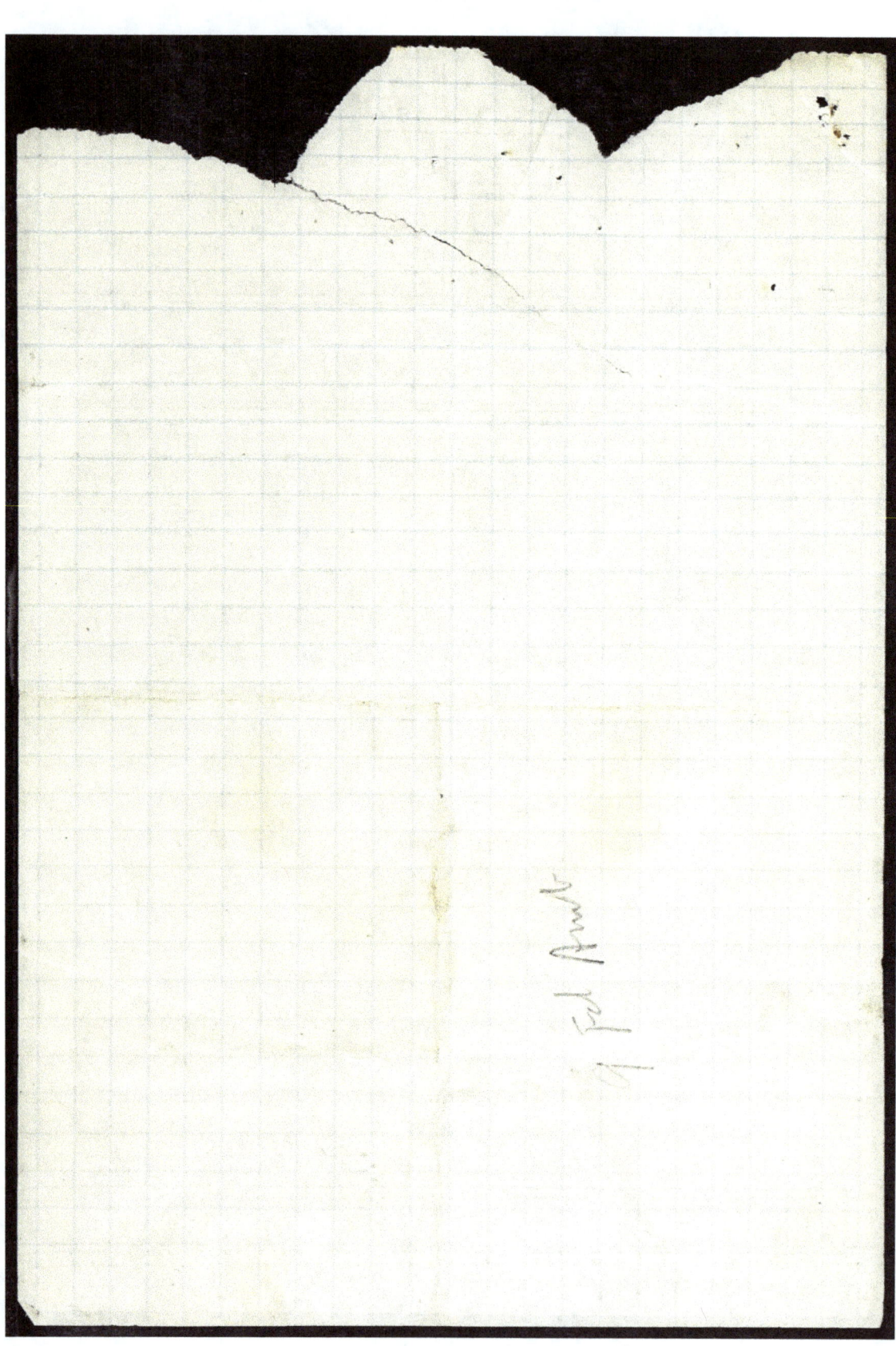

"A" Form.   Army Form C.

MESSAGES AND SIGNALS.   No. of Message

Prefix Code m.	Words	Charge	This message is on a/c of:	Recd. at m.
Office of Origin and Service Instructions	Sent			Date
	At m.		Service	From
	To			
	By		(Signature of "Franking Officer.")	By

TO — 86 y Field Amb

| Sender's Number | Day of Month | In reply to Number | AAA |
| M 346 | 16th Oct 1914 | | |

Move your Field Amb. to road junction on the VIEILLE-CHAPELLE road one & half miles North East of the village

From .... Hexner
Place .... 3 Division
Time

The above may be forwarded as now corrected.   (Z)

                                    Censor.   Signature of Addressee or person authorised to telegraph in his name

Ans

Co. g. Field Ambulance.

Vol IV

15/9/25
Mar. 1914
S/

No 9 Field Ambulance

WAR DIARY
INTELLIGENCE SUMMARY

Army Form C. 2118.

Hour, Date, Place	Summary of Events and Information	Remarks and references to Appendices
10pm 1/14 LA CLYTTE	Ready to move at 6.30 am. No fresh orders. Major STEELE A.D.M.S. 2nd Cav: Division came and handed over some surgical stores to him as he was getting short. I wonder and 2 or 3 sick picked up. These new men from Lincoln & the 3 ambers and most of them were in a very exhausted state. In view of their condition it is unreasonable to send them down to get a rest in a Convalescent Camp before going back to duty. 10 am. received orders to go at once to KEMMEL and assist the Cav: Fd Ambulance than sent on Major HUDLESTON and Capt HABGOOD to KEMMEL to all about some London Scottish wounded said to be there. On our way I met him and knew that we went to proceed to LA CLYTTE instead, as it was expected that KEMMEL would be shelled at any moment, much delay in much owing to the congested condition from traffic. Marched LA CLYTTE about 3 pm. School into for dressing station near church in a farm. Dressing Station quickly got ready and wounded came in almost at once in our wagons which had been out with Capts ROBERTS & FRASER, and all RAMC subunits in Collecting wounded. About 18 cases in all very severe gswds

WAR DIARY
INTELLIGENCE SUMMARY.
(Erase heading not required.)

Army Form C. 2118.

Hour, Date, Place	Summary of Events and Information	Remarks and references to Appendices
1st (Continued)	severe brought in), 3 abdominal with intestines hanging out. An interesting Regimental Doctor as a last resource had died in Dressing Station of G.S. wound of head. The Motor convoy arrived and evacuated part of our wounded, their H. Qrs is BAILLEUL, 3rd Army Corps. 9 p.m. another Case G.S. wd. Abdomen died in Dressing Station. Capt ROBERTS went to H.Qrs of Rifle returning about 9 p.m. having got into touch with them and ascertained that we could not do anything more than had been done with regard to bringing in our 50 officers and 20 men reported to be left in the advanced trenches in advance of WYTSCHAETE. These trenches are now reported to be left in the advanced trenches in advance of WYTSCHAETE. These trenches are now occupied by French Infantry.	
6pm 5th LA CLYTTE	8 a.m. Capt ROBERTS proceeded to b. dl. Stn. to find out position of affairs; no orders except: remain where we are. Motor convoy arrived at 10 a.m. and evacuated the remainder of our wounded, also 2 French officers and 1 man of London Scottish we had collected, obtained 9 more stretchers from them as there is a great shortage of stretchers & blankets owing to the constant wastage	Std

WAR DIARY or INTELLIGENCE SUMMARY

Army Form C. 2118.

Hour, Date, Place	Summary of Events and Information	Remarks and references to Appendices
2/14 (continued)	leakage down to the Clearing Hospitals with no regular replacements. 3pm took over School buildings and Nunnery Station on their being evacuated by 2nd Cav: 3rd Ambulance, the buildings we had taken on previously not having been satisfactory in size and cleanliness. Near 2nd Divn HdQrs moved up to a place 8 miles S.W. Bicycle orderly returned from there with orders to report himself personally with the unit. Have now no information as to what field formation we belong to either than the Brigade.	Sgd.
6 Km S/W, about 1, no dawn BAILLEUL-NIEPPE road	German aeroplane making reconnaissance over our position, near no being a large number of French Cavalry. Shortly after whilst began to drift rear and as no orders had come, and as no British troops were in our front I decided to vacate our position and report what action I had taken to Head Quarters. We left at and proceeded towards LOCRES, on the way Capt ROBERTS whom I had sent on to Hd Qrts got there with a message returned with orders to follow in rear of Brigade to BAILLEUL where we should go into billets. Reached there about 1-30 pm	Sgd.

WAR DIARY
INTELLIGENCE SUMMARY.
(Erase heading not required.)

Army Form C. 2118.

Hour, Date, Place	Summary of Events and Information	Remarks and references to Appendices
5/11/1914 (Continued)	1-30 p.m. and marched through the town to billets at a farm in tram for the men and in some cottages for the Officers about 1.M. down on the BAILLEUL—NIEPPE road. Went to Brigade Office and found men were not allowed to go into the town. Intercut to replace one detachment but spare parts had been taken and Montario were broken in transit. During the days march we crossed French territory at at point about	Smith.
6 p.m. 4th BAILLEUL	2.M. E of NEUVE EGLISE Visited by a D and 3rd Divn who informed that 5 remounts were wanting for the Unit at LESTREM: sent Sergt CHURCH and 4 men A.S.C. to bring these horses up. They were sent by motor. Horses about where necessary. Pt ELKINGTON and party who had been sent for duty to No 6 Clearing H ELKINGTON proton to C. Section, weather fairly hot returned last night and reported for duty. heat turning to rain. Latter part of day.	Smith.

Army Form C. 2118.

WAR DIARY
or
INTELLIGENCE SUMMARY.
(Erase heading not required.)

Hour, Date, Place	Summary of Events and Information	Remarks and references to Appendices
6/11 BAILLEUL	Overhauled wagons and equipment, submitted indents to complete, marking the requirements in order of urgency. Sergt CHURCH. A.S.C. arrived with 8 Remounts and reported that he had been placed under open arrest by a Sergt of Military Police at ESTAIRES charged with being drunk and encouraging gambling amongst natives in a Café. He denied the charge and produced evidence of 4 men who were with him in support of his statement. 4 Heavy draught and 4 light were selected from the mint and 407 Field Ambulance notified of the arrival of the order. 3 Lgy Wom. Shoeing of Horses completed. Regiments of B.W. refitted with surgical supplies &c. this arranged through 9 Field Ambs, at a personal interview. About dropped by Taube Plane in opposite field near aeroplane Spies. Received orders to march at F.1.5am tomorrow to YPRES via LOCRE and DICKEBUSCH.	G.O.M.

Army Form C. 2118.

WAR DIARY
INTELLIGENCE SUMMARY.
(Erase heading not required.)

Instructions regarding War Diaries and Intelligence Summaries are contained in F.S. Regs., Part II. and the Staff Manual respectively. Title pages will be prepared in manuscript.

Hour, Date, Place	Summary of Events and Information	Remarks and references to Appendices
11.30pm - 6/11 ON ROAD YPRES — YLAMERTINGHE	6.30 a.m. received orders to push on to march till 11 p.m. orders given accordingly at 8.45 a.m. orders received from W. Bn. 9th Brigade to march at 10 a.m. Fell in 9.30 a.m. and proceeded to Brigade in BAILLEUL. Proceeded on the LOCRE road. Saw C.O. and about 2 miles out who informed me that for the present return to him shortly. he sent by [first?] of his travelled to send by orderly's numerous halts on the way owing to the congested and bad condition of the roads; passed through LE CLYTTE and DICKENBUSCH; about 1 mile from the latter place on the road to YPRES we turned at point 2 and proceeded in a N.W. direction to the first crossroads where we turned into a field and concealed our wagons as well as possible with branches of trees and by getting under trees where possible and awaited orders from Brigade. N.B. No orders received, waited about 6.30 p.m. When 13th line B'de Regimental transport which was on the same field moved off. we followed. On nearing YPRES the place was being heavily shelled with big guns. At about 11 p.m. met Capt POTTS. R.A.M.C. with No. 7 Field Ambulance who informed me that he had been turned back as the place was [not?] safe to go into. Sent on a cycle orderly who	Smith

WAR DIARY
INTELLIGENCE SUMMARY.

Hour, Date, Place	Summary of Events and Information	Remarks and references to Appendices
6/14 (Continued)	who came back and informed me that a Sergt of Military Police had told him we could not take the Ambulances in and that he did not know where 9th Brigade H.Qrs were. I turned the wagons and marched back to VLAMERTINGHE, having failed to find Tuille Head.; put men on a Brewery. Officers in wagons by the side of the road.	M.A.
11 pm 7/14 VLAMERTINGHE.	6.30 am. sent off a Cycle orderly to D.D.M.S. 1st Corps reporting whereabouts and asking for orders and position of 9th Brigade. 8.30 a.m. sent Delyrum to D.D.M.S. 1st Corps asking for same information; stood fast awaiting orders. 12.30 p.m. no orders. About 5 p.m. order from A.D.M.S. 2nd Division that we were not required and should stand fast, later a message from 1st A Corps by Capt COLLINS that we should send bearers and necessary wagons to HOOGE and remainder to report to 3rd Div Train, a little later a message from 9th Bde W.T. Offr. (no time on it) ordering bearers and wagons to HOOGE after dark and to remain myself in vicinity of KRUISSTRAT, which place it that time not being stated and there being two of them about 1½ m. apart. As orders so conflicting sent Capt FRASER forward first to Dressing Station in YPRES where he ascertained	M.A.

Army Form C. 2118.

WAR DIARY
or
INTELLIGENCE SUMMARY.
(Erase heading not required.)

Instructions regarding War Diaries and Intelligence Summaries are contained in F.S. Regs., Part II. and the Staff Manual respectively. Title pages will be prepared in manuscript.

Hour, Date, Place	Summary of Events and Information	Remarks and references to Appendices
4/11/14 (continued)	ascertained that casualties of 9th Brigade were being collected by their bearers and being dealt with there, next on to 3rd Divn. H.Qrs who told him to see O th' Bde I.O. Drs and inform them what arrangements had been made. He then proceeded to 9 Bde I.O. Qrs and told them where 9th 3rd Ambulance was and what arrangements had been made by 1st Army Corps for their wounded. He returned at 1.10 a.m. and reported what he had done. At 6.10 a.m. I sent off telegram to a 9nd & 3rd Divn reporting this and our whereabouts, and asking if there were any further orders or if me were to stand fast at VLAMERTINGHE.	AWH
11 am 8th VLAMERTINGHE.	3.30 p.m. arranged about evacuating 6 sick men by motor Ambulance, 3.45 p.m. saw Da.Q.M.S. 3rd Divn and explained to him about the orders above referred to, 5 p.m. message from G.O.M.S. 3rd Divn asking about the contradicting orders and saying we should not be required to move before the next day. 10.30 p.m. received orders from a 9 and 3rd Divn to move the next day to KRUISSTRAAT there being two places of this name near together; verbal message sent by despatch rider asking for information as to which was meant.	SWH

Army Form C. 2118.

WAR DIARY
or
INTELLIGENCE SUMMARY.
(Erase heading not required.)

Instructions regarding War Diaries and Intelligence Summaries are contained in F.S. Regs., Part II. and the Staff Manual respectively. Title pages will be prepared in manuscript.

Hour, Date, Place	Summary of Events and Information	Remarks and references to Appendices
6pm. 9/11/14 VLAMERTINGHE	12.35am m/c received message saying at once the KRUISSTRAAT. S.W. of YPRES having the word "lock" printed under. Sent Capt. FRASER, Lieut. CARBERRY and cycle orderly off early in the morning to select billets and send back orderly with message. Capt. FRASER sent back orderly to acquaint me to billets, on arrival found they consisted of straw shelters in a field, houses were occupied by refugees and French officers except 2 or 3 part of town which was reported to shell fire. Sent Capt. FRASER to A.D.M.S. to get some definite orders as to what he wanted done there. In the meantime French artillery officer claimed the shelters belonging to his ammunition column and he said the position was not safe. I moved the unit up the road crossing immediately S of the Chateau in the YPRES– VLAMERTINGHE road and halted there. At 2.30 Capt. FRASER arrived with orders to open a dressing station of one section, and with our teams to clear the wounded at 9th & 15th Batteries over the YPRES–HOOGEMONT and the area around ZILLEBEKE. Divided unit up, all teams & C'Section sent up on arrival under Major HUDLESTON to form dressing station & remainder with H.Q. Quarters. I sent back under command of Lieut. CARBERRY to VLAMERTINGHE. I then went with Major HUDLESTON to search for a site first at the BRIELEN road all houses full of French troops then along VLAMERTINGHE–YPRES road but not finding any suitable site we turned back down the road to KRUISSTRAAT and chose an Estaminet as a dressing station at the road junction just N of the K of KRUISSTRAAT (lock.) Jarrayes with S.M.	

WAR DIARY or INTELLIGENCE SUMMARY.

Army Form C. 2118.

Hour, Date, Place	Summary of Events and Information	Remarks and references to Appendices
9th (Continued)	Major HUDLESTON to billet the men in cottages near and went back to see about J.P.B., found our billets of previous night taken so had 3 tents pitched for personnel.	SW
6 p.m. 10th VLAMERTINGHE	9.30 a.m. A.D.M.S. came over to hear what information had been made. I gave him desired information. 10 a.m. went over to KRUISSTRAAT to advanced dressing station and found that all clearing of wounded had been carried out by No 3 2nd Ambulance the previous night and that only two cases had been taken in. Ordered Bearer Subdivision of 'B' Section and 3 Ambulance wagons to return to H. Quarters as Major HUDLESTON thought we had more men than were needed at Advanced Dressing Station. Ordered men to be put in tents as no billets available. 6 p.m. 13 stretchers and 3 bales of blankets received the latter from Red Cross Society. Lieut: TULLOCH reported for duty from No.6 Clearing Hospital, posted him to 'A' Section to complete establishment. Inspected horses and harness of sections at J.P.Q. & interviewed A.D.V.S. who considered the horse of the unit to be in a very satisfactory state. A.D.M.S. called and went to Advanced Dressing Station with me. Everything there seen satisfactory arrangements	SW
6 p.m. 11th/14th VLAMERTINGHE		Ayd.

WAR DIARY
INTELLIGENCE SUMMARY

Army Form C. 2118.

Hour, Date, Place	Summary of Events and Information	Remarks and references to Appendices
11-11-14 (Continued)	Arranged with Major HUDLESTON re collection of wounded this evening in attack have been made on the portion of our line today held by 9th and 15th Brigades. 13 more stretchers arrived. And all stretchers at D.H. D.Rs. wanted today. All local requisitions are now being paid for in amount impressed of 500 francs from Requisitioning Officer 9th Infantry Brigade this arrangement appears satisfactory but entails much more work for the Quarter Master.	F.M.
6pm 12 7/hr VLAMERTINGHE.	Heavy firing last night with enemy brought off a new determined attack without success. Went over to Advanced Dressing Station at 10-30 am. Found that wounded last night had been all collected under arrangement with Major HOOPER (No 3 3rd Ambce) but he required more Ambulance wagons for tonight as some of his have been damaged. This arranged with Major HUDLESTON. Arranged for all stretchers at Advanced Dressing Station to be washed. Sent urgent memo to A.D.M.S. re clothing for men which is in a very bad state. No orders re; a more position much engaged apparently. two wounded and one sickman evacuated. Some difficulty experienced in getting enough hay for the horses from local sources. Rediced and Sergeant equipment of Unit complete except for minor things.	F.M.
6pm 13 3/hr VLAMERTINGHE.	Brigade Requisitioning Officer called last night and arranged that owing to difficulty in getting forage locally, he would defer approval compressed hay for the unit. Saw A.D.M.S. 10 am, who came to enquire	F.M.

WAR DIARY
INTELLIGENCE SUMMARY.
(Erase heading not required.)

Army Form C. 2118.

Hour, Date, Place	Summary of Events and Information	Remarks and references to Appendices

1.30 a.m. (continued) — enquire if hotel was being arranged for satisfactorily. The man of R. Innis. Regt. brought here last night said to be a spy; he had been behaving in a peculiar manner, papers examined, a map and some papers belonging to a German found. To me he appeared to be feigning mental disease, kept under observation last night and handed over to the Military Police this morning. Warned medical officer if sent about men reporting sick who had left their units without permission, and gave orders that they should be detained, carefully examined, and if nothing found wrong handed over to Military Police for return to their units, with a note of the facts. 11 a.m. sent Lieut WILSON to advanced dressing station to see if anything was required there. Dr. Macks and I intended for Control Detained. 2.15 p.m. A.D.M.S. came over to POPERINGHE to see if any of the ordnance stores already ordered we advanced dressing station to move to the Asylum just about of YPRES on the PLAMERTINGHE-YPRES road. N. of the road. Sent Lieut. CARBERY to see if building available. This was found to be so and "C" Section with N.C. Bearers moved there about 4 p.m. and established a new dressing station. Only a few wounded came in during the night.

6 p.m. 16th/17th VLAMERTINGHE. — Sent Lieut. TOULOCH to DICKENBUSCH to take over a draft of 20 R.C.D. and new reinforcements and bring them up to 1st C.S. Went over to Adv. Dressing Station at YPRES and found everything satisfactory, cleared small rooms

WAR DIARY
INTELLIGENCE SUMMARY

Hour, Date, Place	Summary of Events and Information	Remarks and references to Appendices
11th (Continued).	rooms and a large amount of space in broad corridors. One good room had been taken over as a dressing room. The magno and personal two officers were billetted in the farm belonging to the building. Gave orders that "A" Section Reserve Squadron should return to Items and "B" Section Cyclists go out for duty. Made a re-arrangement of the officers as follows:— "A" Section. Major BLISS, Capt FRASER, Lieut CARBERY, Lieut CONWAY, 192 Mt. "B" " Capt ROBERTS, Lieut TULLOCH, Lieut WILSON. "C" " Major HUDLESTON, Capt HABGOOD, Lieut ELKINGTON. New draft arrived. Inspected them and allotted them to their sections. Made some re-arrangements of mounting horse to fit in with the new postings of officers. Sent to DICK-ENBUSCH for Ordnance Stores but only got 12 Stretchers & 4 packs of medicine. Stores arrived from Advanced Depôt nearing Store POPERINGHE not yet examined.	SM
4pm. 15th/x VLAMERTINGHE.	Weather very cold and wet; some snow. Orders received from about to take Lieut SAINSBURY Rumble (emp. Com) on the strength of the unit and one first one officer to Royal Irish ??? Rifles. Informed O.C. 7th Field Ambulance the above orders and ordered Lieut. TULLOCH to report to O.C. R.I. Rifles. 56 ohr/s, 28 Haversacks. 14 Caps, and 8 Haversaks, 11 mess tins, 12 mess tin covers arrived from Ordnance Store. Lieut SAINSBURY did not join before midnight 15/16.	SM

Army Form C. 2118.

WAR DIARY
or
INTELLIGENCE SUMMARY.
(Erase heading not required.)

Instructions regarding War Diaries and Intelligence Summaries are contained in F.S. Regs., Part II. and the Staff Manual respectively. Title pages will be prepared in manuscript.

Hour, Date, Place	Summary of Events and Information	Remarks and references to Appendices
6pm. 16"/11 VLAMERTINGHE.	Wrote 8am. to L/Cpl Motor Convoy VLAMERTINGHE asking if he could arrange to evacuate sick and wounded daily as I experienced difficulty in getting this done. I had been sending an N.C.O. daily to the Motor rendezvous at the Church, to let the convoy people know that I had sick, and their members sometimes an ambulance was sent, at other times not. He came if breaking out of billets afterwards is very prevalent, a batch of prisoners brought up this morning charged with this offence (nightly refused warning) severely dealt with. Notification received from O.A.D.D. 2nd Div that 2.3 reinforcements should be at DICKEBUSCH and that he went SPINSBURY should return to ROUEN. D.A.D. Sgt WATTS sent to bring up the reinforcements. D.A.D. and S called to arrange matters about taking wounded into our advance dressing station to relieve No. 3 Fd. Ambulance which will probably be replaced by No. Murphy. Arranged for Motor Ambulance to come from A.D. and 3rd Div. daily to evacuate our sick, D. M. Sergt WATTS returned about 5.15 pm. stating that the reinforcements had not arrived yet. Sent N.C.O. to meet reinforcements but 12 men turned up having been sent by D.A. and 3rd Div. Went over to advanced Dressing Station. I found one horse had been serious wounded the previous evening by shell fire when collecting wounded; no casualties amongst personnel. About 35 wounded were collected. Everything seemed satisfactory though a few shells had fallen in the vicinity of the asylum. Met A.D.M.S. 5th Div. Lent and arranged about change of men and rep of the A.S.C. attached to the unit. The collecting is now being done	N.M.
6pm. 17"/14. VLAMERTINGHE.	with Corps motors or alternating with the returns of No 7. Informed major	N.M.

WAR DIARY
INTELLIGENCE SUMMARY.
(Erase heading not required.)

Army Form C. 2118.

Hour, Date, Place	Summary of Events and Information	Remarks and references to Appendices
17/4 (Continued)	Major HUDLESTON that so far as possible the wounded collected by the Reverney if possible be brought to hog Brewery Station so as to go through the hunts & facilitate evacuation by being on the w. of the town. No ordnance stores arrived today. Would a.D.md. asking if ordnance stores could in future be brought to Camp as I had repeatedly sent a cart and found nothing there. One horse (Bay) brought cast from "C" Section with abscess of leg. The Camp is most uncomfortable being an absolute bog, owing to the waterlogged state of the ground and constant rain.	P.d.
6pm 18th Hr VLAMERTINGHE.	Telegram from D.P. in Lahore Division asking what steps had been taken re change against Sgt. CHURCH, notified that change had not yet been received and that Sergt CHURCH had joined this unit. A few straggling sick and wounded come in daily to Head quarters and being evacuated by motor ambulance wagons. Heavy influenced gun fire most of the night "Sharp features 4" seen from w. road. Received orders from R.A.D. that Rev. FLYNN R.C. Chaplain had been posted to 9th Field Ambulance. Capt. HABGOOD R.A.M.B. (S.R.) who had been with the unit since mobilization sent down with septic finger & lymphangitis. Saw D.a.D.m.S. who informed me that probably the unit would get orders to move tomorrow. 2/3 reinforcements did not arrive. Informed A.D.md. 3rd Brign. of this again. No ordnance stores arrived.	P.d.

WAR DIARY
INTELLIGENCE SUMMARY.
(Erase heading not required.)

Army Form C. 2118.

Instructions regarding War Diaries and Intelligence Summaries are contained in F.S. Regs., Part II. and the Staff Manual respectively. Title pages will be prepared in manuscript.

Hour, Date, Place	Summary of Events and Information	Remarks and references to Appendices
6 pm 19th/1/14 VLAMERTINGHE	Orders to move which had been expected did not arrive. Saw A.D.M.S. who informed me that the move would not take place for the present. Went over to advanced Dressing Station, found all correct there. He shelling yesterday afternoon in the immediate vicinity had been very heavy, but no damage done to the tent. Refilled medical with medical and surgical stores as far as the supplies we had seemed to obtain from Advanced Depot Medical stores would go. It was infinitely completer now in this respect. Weather extremely had snowing all the afternoon. Very Cold.	G.W.M.
6 pm 20th/1/14 WESTOUTRE	Went to unrival uneaus station at 9-30am why I know one man had been wounded by shrapnel coming through the roof of the barn in which he had been sleeping. Sam Sergeant and gave order for the unit less 6 ambulances wagons to march at 2 p.m. to WESTOUTRE or else if a suitable place was found to HERSEKEN and to find billets and go into them. Ordered Lieut. CARBERY on two hours in advance to select billets. The horse wounded two days ago is so lame that I am sending him to the mobile veterinary section for treatment. I informed the A.D.M.S. of this fact. He is magnificent to	G.W.M.

WAR DIARY
or
INTELLIGENCE SUMMARY.

Army Form C. 2118.

Hour, Date, Place	Summary of Events and Information	Remarks and references to Appendices
20th (continued)	to the advanced Dressing Station of No.14 Ft Ambulance on the YPRES—MENIN road. to take over some H.D. & SD detained cases and to bring them on to our billets to rejoin their units from there. Marched from VLAMERTINGHE at 2 p.m. the other portion of the unit joining us at that hour, marched via OUDRE DOM—ZEVE COTEN—RENINGHELST HENSKER to WESTOUTRE reaching there at 4 p.m. met A.D.M.S. who informed me that the unit must find billets on one of the main roads running N. from the HESHKEN— WESTOUTRE road. Found a farm ½ m. from the village of WESTOUTRE and billeted the men for the night.	Good
6 p.m. 21.14 BERTHEN.	In the early hours of the morning officers & attendants arrived with men and said they had been ordered to occupy these billets, no about 9 a.m. I referred the matter to 3rd Divn. Staff and was told to proceed to BERTHEN and obtain billets there and use the authority of G.O.C.— 3rd Divn. for obtaining them if necessary. Went on an advance & hunted about for billets. Finally had to share school with 7th Field Ambulance and put "B" Section and "C" Section tent subdivn in a farm ½ mile N.W. from the School and all the transport in a field near the school. Sharick and wounded went bulright on	Fut.

WAR DIARY or INTELLIGENCE SUMMARY

Army Form C. 2118.

Hour, Date, Place	Summary of Events and Information	Remarks and references to Appendices
21/11/14 (continued)	m. 9 of these were evacuated on a motor ambulance and a note sent to O/C Motor Ambulance Convoy asking him to evacuate the rest as I had no accommodation for them. Sent message to 3rd Cav 9th Bde saying where I was and that arrangements would be made by A.D.M.S. 3rd Div. for the evacuation of daily sick, and that I would examine any urgent cases. Very great difficulty experienced in obtaining sufficient billeting accommodation. A convoy arrived about 5.30 pm and took away some 56 wounded & sick to BAILLEUL.	fid.
6pm 22/11 BERTHEN.	Cold with hard frost and some snow on the ground. Went up to Farm to see the position of the unit billetted there. All seemed comfortable. Saw A/Pd on my return and arranged with him to get a motor lorry to come and evacuate sick from units of 9th Brigade and these detained here for evacuation. Convoy came about 3pm & was sent on to collect. Went round Camp and saw that the men in tents had more straw and an extra blanket. Chaplain held parade Impressionary services 8 am. sent memo to M.O. of units of Brigade asking for returns of cases for evacuation. 10 a.m. Motor Convoy arrived.	fid.
6pm 23/11 BERTHEN.		fid.

WAR DIARY
INTELLIGENCE SUMMARY.
(Erase heading not required.)

Army Form C. 2118.

Hour, Date, Place	Summary of Events and Information	Remarks and references to Appendices
23/11/14 (Continued)	arrived and evacuated all the cases we had in. a.10 m/s 3rd Divn arrived and informed me that two officers at a time could go on leave. Selected Major HUDELSTON and Capt ROBERTS and wrote an application for the leave, 2 p.m. sent ambulance wagons to collect the daily sick of units who arrived about 4 p.m. and convoy again arrived at 5 p.m. Evacuated them. Two horses lame, two 3.D. deficient and Kidney deficient; the horse ridden by the Chaplain which had to be shot the day the advanced dressing Station was left at YPRES as it had injured itself. It was first seen by a Veterinary officer who said it must be shot. Regiment still Brigade were supplied with medical equipment and surgical stores to replace deficiencies. A large amount of Ordnance Stores arrived from WESTOUTRE, wearer belts and forty, and ground sheets, making Transport difficult. Major HUDELSTON Saddles on arrival "3 Hampton Terrace, Edinburgh", Captain ROBERTS "89 Hamilton Terrace, London. N.W."	P.M.

Army Form C. 2118.

WAR DIARY
or
INTELLIGENCE SUMMARY.
(Erase heading not required.)

Instructions regarding War Diaries and Intelligence Summaries are contained in F. S. Regs., Part II. and the Staff Manual respectively. Title pages will be prepared in manuscript.

Hour, Date, Place	Summary of Events and Information	Remarks and references to Appendices
6 pm. 24/11, BERTHEN.	Message despatched to O.C. Motor Convoy giving 50 as number for evacuation. Two ambulance wagons sent to collect sick from 9th Brigade units; they were stuck on the road for a long time owing to slippery condition of road. O.C. 2/by A.C. came to see transport, showed him the sick horses and arranged with him for visit from Divl. Train Veterinary Officer; made preparations for more detained sick in the dressing station. Made certain Leave Rands of Corporals and privates rude Order Book of today. Saw A/Dofm.?? and arranged with him re the dressing station to be formed at LA CLYTTE and LOCRE during the next ten days. Obtained some letter billets for the officers of the unit. The present arrangements for evacuation of daily sick is 9th 2 Ambulance collects from units to BERTHEN, from there to BAILLEUL by Motor Ambulance Convoy.	Svd.

WAR DIARY

INTELLIGENCE SUMMARY.
(Erase heading not required.)

Army Form C. 2118.

Instructions regarding War Diaries and Intelligence Summaries are contained in F.S. Regs., Part II. and the Staff Manual respectively. Title pages will be prepared in manuscript.

Hour, Date, Place	Summary of Events and Information	Remarks and references to Appendices
6 p.m. 25th, BERTHEN.	Sent estimate for 60 sick for evacuation to O.C. S/Motor Ambulance Convoy, the numbers being evacuated daily are high, but as there is no suitable accommodation here for men requiring a week or so of rest or treatment there is no alternative. Motor Ambulance Convoy came about 3pm and evacuated 14 sick. These men were carefully sorted out and considered not likely to be fit for some little time. 19 men were detained. Rev: FLYNN, R.C. chaplain reported from ST OMAR for duty with the Unit.	M.
6 p.m. 26th. BERTHEN.	Sick for evacuation about 30, saw ADMS arranged about same for Dr. Hooter and about the BERTHEN—WESTOUTRE road being open for to and fro traffic for Ambulance wagons, it having been closed for to traffic of other motors. Arranged about future site for ambulance when making open. No Ordnance Stores arrived this morning. Called attention	G.W.A.

WAR DIARY
or
INTELLIGENCE SUMMARY.

(Erase heading not required.)

Army Form C. 2118.

Hour, Date, Place	Summary of Events and Information	Remarks and references to Appendices
26th (Continued)	attention of R.O.M.S. to the delay in getting shirts for the men, there still being some 65 men who have not received a new shirt. 3 new ordnance and medical Stores arrived also two new ambulance wagons unit horses complete. The wagons are new it. One new water cart. There are in replacement of defective ones. Both wagons posted to "A" Section.	S/M/S
6pm. 27th/14 BERTHEN.	Allotted new horses to sections and made re distribution where it was necessary. present requirements 2 H.O. Riding. The horses now in the unit are a very satisfactory lot. a B/md arrived, pointed out to him the need for a Convalescent Camp at some place near to save the large number of men suffering from minor ailments, such as sore feet, exhaustion &c. from being sent down the line of communication; there is no accommodation here	S/M/S

WAR DIARY
INTELLIGENCE SUMMARY.
(Erase heading not required.)

Army Form C. 2118.

Hour, Date, Place	Summary of Events and Information	Remarks and references to Appendices
27th (Continued)	sent to obtain the men in the place and no suitable building is available. Also pointed out the need for a dental surgeon to repair dentures and attend to teeth near the front. The Divisional G.O.C. paid a visit and the above requirements were also brought to his notice and met with a sympathetic response, and he promised to see what could be done in the matter after referring it to the A.D.M.S. for his views and recommendations. Notified 9th Bde. ½ Bn. 6th Bn. of the arrangements made for their evacuation of wounded by No. 9 F. Ambce. now they are occupying the trenches again. Received memo from A.D.nd ordering No. 96 Evacuated Daily sick from 6th Bde at WESTOUTRE. Lieut CONWAY(?) on boat proceeded on 7 days leave to England this evening. weather warmer but uncertain, some rain. Shirts have now arrived in sufficient number to give to all men of the unit.	Fwd.

Army Form C. 2118.

WAR DIARY
INTELLIGENCE SUMMARY
(Erase heading not required.)

Instructions regarding War Diaries and Intelligence Summaries are contained in F.S. Regs., Part II. and the Staff Manual respectively. Title pages will be prepared in manuscript.

Hour, Date, Place	Summary of Events and Information	Remarks and references to Appendices
4pm. 28th BERTHEN.	10-30am. inspected all men to see what their requirements were as regards winter clothing &c. One Officer and 1 man wounded and 16 sick evacuated also one case of 3rd degree of frost bite. Visited by A.D.M.S. who informed me of future arrangements for evacuation of wounded. Sent 4 "cast" horses to Mobile Veterinary Section. Two ambulance wagons and one water cart returned to store at BAILLEUL as useless.	S/M.
4pm. 29th. BERTHEN.	Some medical stores arrived, no ordnance stores. Visited billets at farms and found everything satisfactory. One riding horse arrived making the unit complete except for 2 H.D. horses. Leave for Self and Lieut: CARBERY sanctioned.	S/M
4pm. 30th, BERTHEN,	Leave for Rev. ROWAN sanctioned from 2nd to 11th inclusive. Three cases of absence without leave dealt with. 1 dying and 27 sitting cases reported to O.C. Motor ambulance Convoy	S/M.

WAR DIARY
or
INTELLIGENCE SUMMARY.
(Erase heading not required.)

Army Form C. 2118.

Hour, Date, Place	Summary of Events and Information	Remarks and references to Appendices
30/11/14 (Continued)	Convoy for evacuation. Sent Capt Fraser to WESTOUTRE to make a sanitary inspection there of billets occupied by troops. Am sending daily to Ordnance Stores. Weather cold and dull. Health of men is satisfactory. The drinking shops in the town have all been closed by Senior Officer in billets here. Complaint made by C.R.A. that men of ADS attached to 9th Field Ambulance had been cutting down a tree in the field where they are camped, found on investigation that his own men had cut down another tree and that my men seeing this followed their example. Stringent orders issued against cutting hedges and trees without permission.	

G W Nix
Major R am C
OC 9th Field Ambulance.

12/39 b7
Dec. 1914.
La b6/21

Amb

S/ No 9. Field Ambulance.

Vol V.

Army Form C. 2118.

WAR DIARY

No. 9 Field Ambulance

INTELLIGENCE SUMMARY.
(Erase heading not required.)

December 1914.

Hour, Date, Place	Summary of Events and Information	Remarks and references to Appendices
6pm 1/12/14. BERTHEN.	Major BLISS, Lieut. CARBERY and Rev. RONAN proceeded on 4 days leave. Took over command.	W. Hudleston Major R.amc
6pm 2/12/14. BERTHEN.	Received Routine Orders by G.O.C. 3rd Division. Copy it. Paras 3 + 4 taken. Three ambulance wagons sent to LOCRE at 5am. to report to B'de. Send On orders for transport of refugees. One Ambulance wagon sent to Ordnance Depot at WESTOUTRE for stores, hent. ELKINGTON ordered to report for duty with R. Scots, hdts in relief of Lieut. THORNE. Cap't FRASER proceeded to WESTOUTRE and LOCRE with Major CHIPPING on sanitary inspection. Number of sick for evacuation 43, of which 12 for convalescent Camp for Major HUDLESTON, Cap't ROBERTS and Cam'o for Major HUDLESTON, Field Allowance claims for Major HUDLESTON, Cap't ROBERTS and FRASER, and Rev FLYNN made out for sig- nature.	M.H.

Army Form C. 2118.

WAR DIARY
INTELLIGENCE SUMMARY.
(Erase heading not required.)

Instructions regarding War Diaries and Intelligence Summaries are contained in F.S. Regs., Part II. and the Staff Manual respectively. Title pages will be prepared in manuscript.

Hour, Date, Place	Summary of Events and Information	Remarks and references to Appendices
6 pm. 3/12. BERTHEN.	A party consisting of 1 Capt & 7 men accompanied by similar party from No. 7 Field Ambulance, the whole under Capt POTTS, proceeded at 10 a.m. for the Kings inspection at LOCRE. Increase of numbers of sick necessitates placing Rever Inspection "A" Section in Oholing Tent, the large school room being occupied by sick. In addition to 45 noted as evacuated yesterday 29 were detained. To-day number of sick is 65 for evacuation and 36 detained. Charge against Sgt CHURCH, A.S.C., dealt with, and case dismissed.	MH
6 pm. 4/12. BERTHEN.	Total sick admitted 48 and 36 remaining, evacuated 28 and 1 officer.	
6 pm. 5/12. BERTHEN.	No. 7 Field Ambulance takes over all sick of rest of 8th Brigade and other units of this area from to-day. Arrangements made for men to send P.O. orders by to-days mail. Application for F.G. Court Martial on Ptes Bowles and Robinson.	MH

WAR DIARY
INTELLIGENCE SUMMARY.
(Erase heading not required.)

Army Form C. 2118.

Hour, Date, Place	Summary of Events and Information	Remarks and references to Appendices
5/12/14 (Continued)	and Robinson applied for, summary of evidence taken by Capt FRASER. Capt FRASER and Pte Wilbraind attached to "B" Section for work at Dressing Station at LOCRE. Two Ambulance wagons from "A" Section attached to "B" Section. One Ambulance wagon to remain permanently at stable of Chateau N E of Km KEMMEL wagon orderly to report to M.O. R.F.A. at that Chateau	M.
6 p.m. 6/14 BERTHEN	9.30 am "B" Section under Capt ROBERTS R.a.m.b left for duty at Dressing Station LOCRE "A" Section travel Sub-Division moved to farm. S/Major GIBBS proceeded on leave last evening. Q.M. Sgt WATTS returned from leave this morning. No.467 Farrier KITSON. A.S.C. reported for duty with No.9 3rd Ambulance from No: 3 Divn'l Supply Column.	
6 p.m. 7/14 BERTHEN	Section wagons, carts & all personnel moved to farm, as standing for horses in original field is very bad.	M.

WAR DIARY
INTELLIGENCE SUMMARY
(Erase heading not required.)

Army Form C. 2118.

Hour, Date, Place	Summary of Events and Information	Remarks and references to Appendices
4/7/17 (Continued)	Memo: to A.D.M.S. re disposal of Farrier KITSON. No: 5/55 Pte BALDWIN. XV Meados detained for dog-bite on 4/7/17. Dog examined by Veterinary Officer 3rd Divisional Ammunition Column, and reported as showing no signs of rabies. Lieut. WILSON relieved Lieut. TULLOCH (by order of the A.D.M.S.) as officer in medical charge of Royal Irish Rifles, the latter reporting himself for duty at the Advanced Dressing Station at LOCRE. Visited Advanced Dressing Station at LOCRE and found everything satisfactory.	M.
6pm 8/7/17 BERTHEN		

WAR DIARY
INTELLIGENCE SUMMARY.
(Erase heading not required.)

Army Form C. 2118.

Instructions regarding War Diaries and Intelligence Summaries are contained in F.S. Regs., Part II. and the Staff Manual respectively. Title pages will be prepared in manuscript.

Hour, Date, Place	Summary of Events and Information	Remarks and references to Appendices
6 p.m. 9/11. BERTHEN.	Arrived back from 7 days leave and took over command from Major HUDLESTON, unit still in billets at BERTHEN but (R)ectors at LOCRE, forming an advanced dressing station. Number of wounded small at present. Evacuation of wounded being carried out by Motor Convoy to BAILLEUL direct. Saw A.D.M.S. and arranged for Lieut. TULLOCH who has not been well lately and has been brought back from duty, with a regiment, to Dressing Station, to return to H.Qrs. and to be replaced by Lieut. CROSBY. Orders having come re building shelters for horses referred to A.D.V.S. for information as to the probable time we should be here to see if the expenditure likely to be entailed was justifiable, selected suitable site in Enc(losure?) answer in positive. Pte Bower & Robinson tried this day of F.G, Chantiel, 180 fur coats and 40 horse rugs decided when Ordnance store received from Oran and Department, this makes the men's clothing pretty nearly complete.	SWA

WAR DIARY / INTELLIGENCE SUMMARY

Army Form C. 2118.

Hour, Date, Place	Summary of Events and Information	Remarks and references to Appendices
6pm. 10/12/1914. BERTHEN	Chose site for horse shelters and moved transport to the farm where most of the men of the unit are billetted. Rev: E.F. CAMPBELL C.F. Chaplain reported his arrival from ROUEN in relief of Rev. Roman proceeding to ROUEN, vacated by a 2nd Lt. Owen; very few casualties at the Dressing Station last night. Quarter-master arranged arrangements for getting the poles, wire & straw for thatching for the horse shelters. The weather wet and mild. Health of men of unit Ruperts good. Notified Capt ROBERTS at the Dressing Station that he should collect sick from Brigade in support now that we are in action and that the Field Ambulance on duty at BERTHEN would only clear the WESTOUTRE area, as there had apparently been some misunderstanding about the areas to be respectively cleared.	
6pm 11/12/14. BERTHEN	Work of building shelters proceeded with. Went with	

WAR DIARY
INTELLIGENCE SUMMARY.
(Erase heading not required.)

Army Form C. 2118.

Hour, Date, Place	Summary of Events and Information	Remarks and references to Appendices
11th (continued)	D.A.D.M.S. to the Dressing Station at HCRE. Accommodation as at present arranged for is only sufficient for retaining daily sick and a few cases of wounds and there is no separate room available for dressing wounded cases in, also the accommodation does not for sick or wounded officers is practically nil. Opinion of officers suffering severely from diarrhoea was in keeping treated in the only room which was available for the medical staff of the ambulance to take their meals in. These points and being brought to the notice of the A.D.M.S 3 men in splinting, 8 english little 12 stretchers and some other Ordnance Equipment received. The horse sick pneumonia of two with laminitis, leaving me with 5 Draught horses not effective. The Rev. R. van Liff for ROUEN today, the amount of Tobacco being received for the men now from Government and Private	G.W.B.

WAR DIARY / INTELLIGENCE SUMMARY

Army Form C. 2118.

Hour, Date, Place	Summary of Events and Information	Remarks and references to Appendices

11th (continued)

is too much. Wrote to ADMS NANTES from whom a large amount had been received informing him that if it was contemplated to send any more presents to the men, milk cocoa or some tinned food articles would be really more useful.

Read out details of 2 F.A. (Ambulances) nightly OC bearing Station that he should return with "B" Section to Y.P.A.D.

6pm. 12th, BERTHEN

Saw ADMS 3rd Divn on various routine matters, pointed out that the Bearing Station at RICRE is not large enough & has no proper accommodation for sick officers other than with our own officers which is at times inadvisable. Also that some serious men were needed to screen of wounded whilst being dressed. Also pointed out the need for reserve rations for feeding sick detained at Bearing Station as at present we have to feed them from RAMC men's rations, As men reporting sick do not bring their day's rations.   GH.

WAR DIARY or INTELLIGENCE SUMMARY

Army Form C. 2118.

Hour, Date, Place	Summary of Events and Information	Remarks and references to Appendices

12/1/16 (Continued)

In spite of orders to that effect, Went to inspect work of making horse shelter and made some further suggestions. Evacuated 45 men and 1 Officer sick to Clearing Station by motor ambulance Convoy, three cases all from Brigade in reserve. Saw Col: BOYLE who complained that he had found RAMC nbr. of No 79 Field Amb. at BOESCHEPPE which was now a French area, and out of bounds for British troops. He gave me an order to have a pioneer on the road short of the village, arranged for this. B Section rejoined the unit at 4 pm. Saw A.D.V.S. and told him that I wanted 6 more draught horses to complete and replace casualties, one horse died of pneumonia today at ZICKE, the large number of men now reporting sick appears to be due to the inclement weather, unhealthy conditions in the trenches, lack of comfort in billets, wet clothing and hardships of the campaign.

GMA.

WAR DIARY / INTELLIGENCE SUMMARY

Army Form C. 2118.

Hour, Date, Place	Summary of Events and Information	Remarks and references to Appendices
April 15/16 BERTHEN	Visited by A.D.M.S. 2nd Div. who informed me that troops might have to move to make room for other units coming into this area. Sent Major HUDLESTON & Lieut CARBERY with billeting staff officer to choose billets in rear area. Have gifts received for the men from private sources of clothing and tobacco. None of these are now being sent out than are required. Orders received to indent for 100 blankets, 200 pyjamas 200 Behaviks, 200 slippers for sick. Wrote around pointing out that no transport is available for carrying them, and asking for an extra country cart to carry them. At present to carry the horings, blankets, ministerial stores & spare dressings which have been issued to the unit we have only two extra light country carts instead of 3 forage carts with two establishments (Transport). The Monmouth (T) Engineers having moved out of a small flour mill next to Meeveny Station, I have moved A. Section Bearer Sub-division in to the billets at the Farm were incorporated. Evacuated 3 lying and 30 sitting cases of sick to Clearing Hospital. Smith.	

WAR DIARY or INTELLIGENCE SUMMARY

Hour, Date, Place	Summary of Events and Information	Remarks and references to Appendices
6pm. 14/4/14 Near WESTOUTRE	Men moved to parade at 4.30 a.m. but seatime difficulty experienced in getting the wagons out of the field, as the weather conditions had been so unfavourable & the ground was so water-logged. Bearers & wagons of B Section under Capts. ROBERTS and FRASER went on in advance to LOCRE. The remainder of unit marched off about 6am for the new billets reaching there about 1 hour later. Settled men in billets & then went on to WESTOUTRE to inspect Dressing Station under Major HUDLESTON. Found it in the school in WESTOUTRE. Accommodation for about 60 sick. No accommodation for Sgt Indentures or Medical officer. Went to R.A.M.C. instructed if they could arrange for one room to be spared for the latter. Interviewed Supply Officer of the Batt re rations which had been rather short, some difficulty is experienced in feeding the sick whose & some of their rations still there as a rule, & it has been found necessary to give them on the rations supplied for Rank personnel. I have also put in a letter to G.H.Q. asking to be allowed to draw 100 spare rations for feeding sick & wounded in the Ambulance. J.A.M.	

Army Form C. 2118.

WAR DIARY
INTELLIGENCE SUMMARY.
(Erase heading not required.)

Hour, Date, Place	Summary of Events and Information	Remarks and references to Appendices
6pm. 15/4/17 Near WESTOUTRE	Excellent work rendered last night by Captains ROBERTS and FRASER Bands with the bearers of B. Section in collecting men of the Gordons & Royal Scots Battalions who were wounded in an attack made on the enemy's position. When it became known that there were a considerable number of wounded up in the area of the trenches, Capt. FRASER & the bearers went right up to the trenches and assisted the Regimental Stretcher Bearers in collecting them and bringing them back to the wagons. I hear unofficially that the G.O.C. was very pleased with the work done. Went down to WESTOUTRE and inspected the Dressing Station under Major HUDLESTON and then on to LOCRE to the main Dressing Station (No.7 F. Amb'ce). Here I met ADMS and arranged to relieve the bearers who had done good work the previous night by three of our stretcher sections detailed Lieut. CARBERY and bearers of "D" section, supplemented by 10 bearers of "B" section to go with 2 wagons of "A" section and 1 of "C" (2 wagons of "A" section being broken.) Capt. ROBERTS & bearers	

SM.

WAR DIARY
INTELLIGENCE SUMMARY.
(Erase heading not required.)

Army Form C. 2118.

Hour, Date, Place	Summary of Events and Information	Remarks and references to Appendices
15/14 (Continued)	of "B" section returned to H.Q.rs. Four officers' patterns at of saddlery received today which had been indented for some months ago. Arrangements have been made to enable the unit to draw up to maximum of 100 rations for use of sick and wounded. These are to be replaced on requisition by accompanying "certificate from O.C. that they have been expended on the sick. Weather remains very unsettled with much rain. Lieut. J.B. WOOD, R.A.M.C. (Temporary Commission) joined at WESTOUTRE today for duty and was taken on the strength of the Unit.	
6pm 16/14 near WESTOUTRE	Went down to WESTOUTRE at 10.30 am and none of sick had come in of which a large number required evacuation. Obtained a room for the officers doing duty there to live in. Arranged for Major HUDLESTON and Lieuts WOOD and WILSON to rejoin Lt. Quarles and for Capt ROBERTS	

WAR DIARY
INTELLIGENCE SUMMARY

Army Form C. 2118.

Hour, Date, Place	Summary of Events and Information	Remarks and references to Appendices
16/7/14 (Continued)	and kent. CARBERY to take over the duties there. Motor Convoy arrived there about 12 noon for unloading etc. Took over room in Salaminé for 3 officers rear Headquarters. Saw fitting of some new saddlery Officers Pattern. Received authority to draw 2 Heavy Draught & Light Draught horse from Divisional Ammunition Column. Officers and men with 3 ambulance wagons returned last evening from the Ordering Station LOCRE, their services being no longer required to escort No. 7 Field Ambulance, 4 p.m. horses above referred to arrived armed and proved to be remounts and very satisfactory ones.	M.S.
6 p.m. 17/7/14 Near WESTOUTRE	Inspected horses & vehicles. Sent to WESTOUTRE to take over rear Ambulance wagon & 1 water cart. These arrived with 2 drivers, harness and horses complete. The horses were moderately good. The Ambulance wagon of new pattern, the water cart of old but	Sgt.

WAR DIARY
or
INTELLIGENCE SUMMARY.
(Erase heading not required.)

Army Form C. 2118.

Hour, Date, Place	Summary of Events and Information	Remarks and references to Appendices

17/14 (Continued) — without any fitting candles. Allotted the horses cart & wagons as follows:— Amb: Wagon "A" Section, Water Cart "A" Section. 2 Heavy draught horses "A" Section, 2 Light draught horses to "B" Section. Pte Kent tried this day by 2 G.C.M. Capt FRASER prosecuting, made some arrangements about the men's Xmas dinner. SADDS came over during the afternoon, brought new Regulations concerning of letters to his notice, asked for his assistance in getting a ruling the order being the mention of number, rank, unit or formation on letters. Have our friends communicate with men coming from other units. 2 Lieut: FLEMING. R. A.m.C. (Camp Comr) joined and was posted to "B" Section. Authority received today for the following promotions (acting) to be made from the date specified. to acting Sergeants:- Corpl Chamberlain 24/14, Corpl W.Crowe 29/14. To acting Corporals Pte Jeffs H, Pte J.C. Watterson, Pte A.J.Buys, Pte J.Bulmore and Pte J.Burton. All from 29/14.

BM.

Army Form C. 2118.

WAR DIARY
INTELLIGENCE SUMMARY.
(Erase heading not required.)

Instructions regarding War Diaries and Intelligence Summaries are contained in F.S. Regs., Part II. and the Staff Manual respectively. Title pages will be prepared in manuscript.

Hour, Date, Place	Summary of Events and Information	Remarks and references to Appendices
17th (Continued)	To be Acting Lance Corporals from 29th inst. P^{te} Grundy, P^{te} Royce, P^{te} Antoniou, P^{te} Radcliffe P^{te} Gough, P^{te} R. T. Taylor.	PM
18th 4pm. Near WESTOUTRE.	Went round with Veterinary Officer inspecting horses. One ordered to sick lines was replaced from the Veterinary Section. Visited Dressing station at WESTOUTRE and found everything alright. Some 70 odd men had reported sick, a large number suffering from effects of cold in feet. Weather very bad, raining most of day and colder. Changed over officers at Dressing Station. This change is being effected every 2 days. Capt FRASER R.A.M.C. is carrying out a Sanitary Inspection of WESTOUTRE area occupied by troops.	PM
19th 6pm. near WESTOUTRE	The unit remains in same situation. Sick rate about the same. Some preparations made for erecting shelters for horses and men. Material arranged for locally. Weather continues wet and rather cold.	PM.

Forms/C. 2118/11.

WAR DIARY or INTELLIGENCE SUMMARY.

Army Form C. 2118.

(Erase heading not required.)

Hour, Date, Place	Summary of Events and Information	Remarks and references to Appendices
6 p.m. 20/12/14 WESTOUTRE.	Visited by A.D.V.S. who inspected all the horses & found one case of mange. Sent off to Mobile Veterinary Section with suspect. Harness was disinfected. Started fixing up the shelters for the horses & collecting material for new shelters. Went down to WESTOUTRE & saw Divisional Station & arranged about personnel having Xmas dinner at WESTOUTRE as they preferred it. Dep. D.M.S. called, settled with him to go on allowing men to Sent 9th Field Ambulance as an address on their letters as otherwise they cannot indicate to their friends where to send an answer. 2nd M. Sgt. Rolfe to go on 7 days leave to ENGLAND tomorrow. Posted Lieut. Wilson to 1 Warwicks, Lieut. Arnott 16th Fus: Lieut. Wood 4th R. Fusiliers, all for one week to permit the M.Os attached to these units to go on one week leave. Tried to get leave for Pte. Hunting R.A.M.C. as a special case. S.M.O.	

WAR DIARY
or
INTELLIGENCE SUMMARY.
(Erase heading not required.)

Army Form C. 2118.

Hour, Date, Place	Summary of Events and Information	Remarks and references to Appendices
20th (Continued)	his mother having died & he being the elect of 6 sons serving. Weather fine, bright & warmer.	
6 P.M. 21st W. WESTOUTRE	Inspected all horses & isolated two to be seen by Veterinary Officer? Mange, then afterwards seen by him & pronounced "Mange". Progress made with horse shelters & stables for the men, went up to see A.D.M.S at Hd. Qrs with Major HUDLESTON. Informed by A.D.M.S. that Major HUDLESTON was to visit a Convalescent Depot in the Schoolroom at BERTHEN for accommodation of 60 men, personnel material to be found by 9th Field Ambulance & supplemental from outside sources. Dining & Recreation rooms to be provided recommendation for 2 Convalescent Officers. Informed A.D.M.S. that tub of clean [?] would be required. Boilers for hot water, bath tubs, hanging lamps extra blankets, Hospital Clothing, slippers, & other of mens clothing being cleansed-dried, & that it would be necessary to make some	M.A. M.A.

WAR DIARY
or
INTELLIGENCE SUMMARY.
(Erase heading not required.)

Army Form C. 2118.

Hour, Date, Place	Summary of Events and Information	Remarks and references to Appendices
21st/11/12 (Continued)	local arrangements for washing & drying the mens clothing. Then visited BERTHEN & found that school was being cleaned out by arrangement of C.R.A., returned Hd Qrs, & made arrangements for Major HUDLESTON, LT: CARBERY & men O'tent dets: Division, & men Bearer Sub: Division with 2 Cooks & complement of N.C.Os, C' Section baggage wagon M.S. Major & Forage cart, to March 10 a.m. tomorrow - march off.	M.S.
6 P.M. 22nd 11th WESTOUTRE.	Inspected work of building shelters for men, horses & found work progressing satisfactorily. Went down to Dressing Station & arranged about commencing entire inoculations. Interviewed G.O.C. 8th Bde. & arranged for the men & officers to go to Dressing Station for inoculation following afternoon. Maj: HUDLESTON, LT: CARBERY party left at 10 a.m. & established Convalescent Depôt at BERTHEN. Informed A.D.M.S. that the windows of the Mess had not been mended in the building to be used	Capt.

WAR DIARY
INTELLIGENCE SUMMARY
Army Form C. 2118.

Hour, Date, Place	Summary of Events and Information	Remarks and references to Appendices
22/12/15 Continued.	Sent Maj: HUDLESTON list of articles which were available at No 8 Field Ambulance & which could be utilised in the Brewing Station. Heard later that an officer R.E. with D.A.D.M.S. had been to Ordnance Dept. in connection with making necessary local & other arrangements. Capt. FRASER has then informed that he is to exercise supervision over the "Bath" arrangements. Weather wet & cold. Arrangements for xmas Christmas dinner proceeding.	End
6.P.M. 28/12/15 WESTOUTRE.	Went down to BERTHEN & saw what had been done at Ambulance Depot, suggested to Major HUDLESTON that more sleeping accommodation be provided & a large room be allotted as Recreation room to be used for this purpose. Went to BAILLEUL with Maj: CHOPPING & bought 6 hanging lamps, 6 buckets, 4 bath tubs & one more hot water boiler. R.E. are fixing up a shed for bathing. Rations being sent direct	End

WAR DIARY or INTELLIGENCE SUMMARY

Army Form C. 2118.

Hour, Date, Place	Summary of Events and Information	Remarks and references to Appendices

23/12 Continued.

by supply lorry. Went to No.2 Clearing Hospital & got staff of Medical Comforts. Shelter for men to be used as dining room & recreation nearly completed. Shelters for horses making satisfactory progress. One horse C. Section had to be shot by order of Veterinary Officer. Temp 108. He's been ill some days. Now require 3 H.D. horses to complete 4 3 H.D. to replace 3 L.D. horses as spares. Many Xmas presents have been received for the men; these are to be distributed on Christmas Day. Inoculation against Enteric being carried out this afternoon at Dressing Station, WESTOUTRE.

SWA

6 P.M. 24/12/14. WESTOUTRE. Wrote A.D.M.S. 3rd Divn asking him to arrange for details in WEST-OUTRE area to be sent to Dressing Station at WESTOUTRE for ambulance. Typhoid inoculation at 2.3 P.M. on 27th inst. Spent the morning making arrangements about mens Christmas dinner viz. Two pigs bought for mens Dinners. Special strong meek bread, batter & plum pudding.

SWA

WAR DIARY
or
INTELLIGENCE SUMMARY.

(Erase heading not required.)

Army Form C. 2118.

Hour, Date, Place	Summary of Events and Information	Remarks and references to Appendices
24/12/14 (Continued.)	& other gifts from people at home. A most excellent shelter has been made by the men, tables have been made with some planks & forms in a similar way.	Gsd
25/12/14. 6 P.M. N° WESTOUTRE	Church Parade 10 a.m. attended by a very large number of the men, made preparation for mens dinners which were served at 1.30. when they were visited by the Officers at Hd.qtrs. PRINCESS MARY'S Gifts did not arrive during the morning but heard at 2.30 they were on their way. H distributed their HER MAJESTY'S Christmas Cards after Church Parade & gave away numerous gifts sent by friends at home for the men. Weather cold & frosty with some mist. The Officers are dining at 6.30 to go over to the menu consult afterwards.	Gsd
26/12/14. 6 P.M. N° WESTOUTRE.	Went down to WESTOUTRE to Dressing Station arranged for more mattresses & for an increase in the accommodation for men detained overnight. Arranged about entrainment of Antyphoid.	Sd.

WAR DIARY or INTELLIGENCE SUMMARY

Army Form C. 2118.

Hour, Date, Place	Summary of Events and Information	Remarks and references to Appendices
26th/12th (Continued)	inoculation on 27th. Came back to Headquarters, saw some of the horses & inspected progress made in building of horse shelters. Afternoon unit paraded to read out finding of F.G.C.M. Order from Gen. C. Went to BERTHEN saw progress made at Convalescent Depot, made certain suggestions re bath room, the floor of which was being made of bricks laid in sand, this appeared to be unsatisfactory as all waste water was run down between & bricks became displaced. Tables have been made for dining room in a very satisfactory manner by some men of the R.A.M.C. Windows are being glazed where broken but it struck me that this work & the work of the Engineers employed was very slow.	
6pm 27th/12th WESTOUTRE	Church parade 10 am, purposes made in fitting up Convalescent Depot at WESTOUTRE. Anti-typhoid inoculation of 70% of Hamb men at WESTOUTRE carried out. After some hard months	S.M.A Sat.

WAR DIARY or INTELLIGENCE SUMMARY.

(Erase heading not required.)

Hour, Date, Place	Summary of Events and Information	Remarks and references to Appendices
Jan 27/12/14 (Continued)	Experience of a Field Ambulance in Summer and Winter. I am of opinion that it is too big a unit. I think 2 sections FA with 10 stretcher squads to each say and the cutting down of a lot of equipment which in my experience is never required would be beneficial. I have sent to ADMS application asking for sanction to return a list of these articles to Ordnance Store as not necessary. The wagons are already too heavily laden and as no separate Forage Cart for section has been supplied for carrying spare blankets, horse rugs, heavy clothing of men when not required unless the wagons already belonging to the unit are lightened we shall not be able to get along the road. SMS	
Jan 28/12/14 Near WESTOUTRE	Went to BERTHEN Convalescent Depot ran by CRE and arranged to get bath room floor covered with zinc sheets, also for Lieut. CARBERY to order 1500 bricks for making hotroak back out	

WAR DIARY
INTELLIGENCE SUMMARY.
(Erase heading not required.)

Army Form C. 2118.

Hour, Date, Place	Summary of Events and Information	Remarks and references to Appendices
28/12/14 (Continued)	of building. Ingoldd to Major HUDLESTON that he wrote Report Board that ordnance stores and supplies had not arrived, also the necessary medical comforts, glazing of windows nearly completed and eating accommodation in diningHall now arranged for with forms. Returned and inspected shelter for horses now completed accommodation for 23 horses. Lieuts AYENT, WOOD & WILSON returned from Temporary duty and reported their arrival at Headquarters. Lieut. WILSON's leave sanctioned as from 28th. Cr. Mr Jr. ROLFE and RQW HARDING came back from leave last night. Leave sanctioned from Rev. CAMPBELL and Rev. Father FLYNN attached to Field Ambulance from 30th Dec to 5th January inclusive. Weather warmer but a good deal of rain. Handed over two rooms in one of our billets for accommodation of Officers of H.A.C. No 7 226/8 Pt J. GILBERT a/Corp attached to 9th Field Ambt.	

WAR DIARY
INTELLIGENCE SUMMARY

(Erase heading not required.)

Army Form C. 2118.

Hour, Date, Place	Summary of Events and Information	Remarks and references to Appendices
28/7/14 (Continued) 10pm	Ambulance was taken and slowly all about 6 or 7pm. Capt FRASER and Lieut. AVENT called and found him practically dead. Artificial respiration resorted to without avail. Court of Inquiry to be held.	Sgd
6pm 29/7/14 Near WESTOUTRE	Notified about of above casualty. Court of Inquiry may held 10.30 a.m. Verdict "Death from natural Causes (syncope the result of acute dilatation of stomach from over distention with a mass of undigested food. A heavy storm last night brought down the new shelter & about 6 horse standings. Went to Hd Qrs 3rd Divn and arranged with A.D.M.S. about a probable move in the near future. Funeral of the man above referred to took place in the Church yard at BERTHEN. Evidence of Court of Inquiry handed over personally to A.D.M.S. A very large number of men reported sick at Dressing Station at WESTOUTRE today, especially South Lancs. About two antityphoid inoculation carried out today at Dressing Station.	Sgd S.M.
6pm. 30/7/14 Near WESTOUTRE	Visited Dressing Station WESTOUTRE and arranged with	Sgd S.M.

WAR DIARY
INTELLIGENCE SUMMARY.
(Erase heading not required.)

Hour, Date, Place	Summary of Events and Information	Remarks and references to Appendices
30th/12 (Continued)	Capt ROBERTS to increase his accommodation for Wounded cases to try and demand the large garage. Shall come suggestions about the treatment of the men coming in with swollen feet (early cases) (telephone to exch) wrote Brigade Major 7th Inf Brigade as increasing accommodation by getting a horse for personnel of Dressing Station to live in. Received reply regretting none to be had & suggesting applying 3rd Division for horsing accommodation. Arranged for 200 kilos straw for Dressing Station. Representative of the Cross Society called, asked him to let me have 25 cents of Pyjamas for use of sick and wounded officers passing through. Major MAURICE 8th Fd Ambulance called to ascertain accommodation in three billets. Showed him round and explained that accommodation would be insufficient for his unit. also informed him of present arrangements at WESTOUTRE. Received notification bus supplied for patient of WO2947 ACP	

Army Form C. 2118.

WAR DIARY
or
INTELLIGENCE SUMMARY.
(Erase heading not required.)

Hour, Date, Place	Summary of Events and Information	Remarks and references to Appendices
30/12/14 (Continued)	Antityphoid Inoculations being still carried on at Sleeping Station. Yesterday's evacuation from Sleeping Station showed 47. Of these 15 were sent to the Convalescent Depot BERTHEN and 25 to ST OMER Convalescent Depot.	SMO
6pm 31/12/14 Rear WESTOUTRE	Went down to Convalescent Depot, suggested asking Red Cross Society for hot sheets, slippers, mats for doors & a few other things required for men's comfort. Went round BERTHEN to find what other accommodation was available for extending the Convalescent Depot, without putting the men into small houses spread about which I consider inadvisable. Could only find suitable accommodation for 43 more men. This would give a total accommodation of about 130. Looked for billets for officers of the Unit as I had heard that the whole would be moving there. Found a dining room at Chateau and bedrooms for an Int. interpreter down to arrange about other billets in the.	SMO

Army Form C. 2118.

WAR DIARY
or
INTELLIGENCE SUMMARY.
(Erase heading not required.)

Hour, Date, Place	Summary of Events and Information	Remarks and references to Appendices
12 31/12/14 (Continued)	afternoon. 4pm received orders to move tomorrow to BERTHEN when relieved by No 8 Field Ambulance and to open a Dressing Station in the school at St JANS CAPPEL for sick. Detailed Capt FRASER Sgt LEWIS, 1 Cpl 6 men Tent sub division 'A' Section with Medical Store wagon, Forage Cart, Water Cart and 1 Ambulance wagon to proceed at 10 am to ST JANS CAPPEL to form a Dressing Station. The rest of unit to parade at 11am to BERTHEN to billets. A fatigue party detailed to clean up and follow on. Capt ROBERTS notified at Dressing Station WESTOUTRE to hand over to No 8 Field Ambulance and follow on.	

End of December 1914.

Geo Alex
Major, Comdg
OC 9th Field Ambulance

3RD DIVISION
MEDICAL

9TH FIELD AMBULANCE
~~JAN-DEC 1915~~

1915 JAN — 1915 JULY

To Guards Div
Aug 1915

8 FIELD AMBULANCE.
1914 AUG TO 1919 MAY.

9 FIELD AMBULANCE.
1914 AUG TO 1915 JULY.

3 Annexures

AMD

121/4256
Jan 1915

9th Field Ambulance
Vol VI

WAR DIARY
INTELLIGENCE SUMMARY.
(Erase heading not required.)

Army Form C. 2118.

9th Field Ambulance

January 1915.

Hour, Date, Place	Summary of Events and Information	Remarks and references to Appendices
6 pm. 1st January/15 BERTHEN	Left billet 9.30 a.m. Went to BERTHEN and allotted billets for men of the unit. Remd. in barns on a farm, All in barns at Mayor's house. Found some billets for horses from which straw had been taken away - these to be restrained. Officers' billet arranged for all Officers in various hotels. G.O.C. & Staff 2nd Division visited Convalescent Depot and seemed very satisfied with what had been done, looked G.O.C. have come into orders to enable more men to be taken in this he promised. I pointed out that the houses in the village were unsuitable for the purpose. Capt. FRASER had been sent on to St. JEAN CAPPEL to start a Becoming Station in the school there. Went over in the afternoon to see this place. Accomodation for about 20 detained cases, men billited in a house next door on either side and Capt FRASER'S accomodation arranged for in Schoolmaster's house. had arrangements about getting coal. Lieut CARBERY sent into BAILLEUL to get crockery and sheets, tablecloths and bedroom ware for sick officers as information had been received that 2 officers were going to be sent for admission. Sir WILLIAM LEISHMAN and Col. BEVERIDGE came to see Convalescent Depot	Sir William Leishman husband OC 9th F. Ambce

Army Form C. 2118.

WAR DIARY
of
INTELLIGENCE SUMMARY.
(Erase heading not required.)

Instructions regarding War Diaries and Intelligence Summaries are contained in F.S. Regs., Part II. and the Staff Manual respectively. Title pages will be prepared in manuscript.

Hour, Date, Place	Summary of Events and Information	Remarks and references to Appendices
1/1/15 (Continued)	and seemed much pleased with what they saw. We proposed that coal be asked for in bulk as the supply in small quantities is uncertain and unsatisfactory.	p.t.o
6am 2/15 BERTHEN	Went round all the men's billets & found them satisfactory. A room taken for Transport Sergeants near horse lines. Some shelter to found ready built & kept by some other unit in rear of the farm where all the men's billets. there were allotted for horses of a Water. A room taken at Salamint close to Convalescent Depot as a store room. Great assistance has been given to the O.C. 9/15 in organising by the O. Nr. 9, 3/Ambulance who is for the present taking over all the "stores" under one roof and arranging to issue as required to 2/15. Went to St JEAN APPEL. Found all as satisfactory at the Dressing Station there, so rode attaimed. Capt. ROBERTS & Lieut WOOD went Sub-Division of "B" Sector with 2 ambulance wagons and other wagons of the section arrived at 4 p.m. from WESTOUTRE having handed	p.t.o

WAR DIARY
INTELLIGENCE SUMMARY
(Erase heading not required.)

Army Form C. 2118.

Hour, Date, Place	Summary of Events and Information	Remarks and references to Appendices
2/15 Continued	the Dressing Station there to No 8 Field Ambulance, then allotted billets, also officers. Lieut WOOD warned to go to ST. JEAN CAPPEL tomorrow to take over Dressing Station from Capt FRASER now in Command. Arranged for the Refugees to live in two rooms, that chateau the other at a house where Capt ROBERTS & Capt FRASER are billetted, as the accommodation is not enough for one large room at either house. Went to see work going on in horse shelters & improvements made satisfactorily. Interviewed O/C Srd Supplies arranged to draw all supplies for Unit as well as for Convalescent Depot from Divisional Supply Column, made arrangements about drawing Coal & paraffin from same source giving 4 days notice beforehand. Brought Capt FRASER in from Dressing Station. ST JEANS CAPPEL & replaced him by Lieut WOOD.	
6pm 3/15 BERTHEN	Orders received for Bearer Sub-Division of 1 Section and	SW

WAR DIARY or INTELLIGENCE SUMMARY

Army Form C. 2118.

Hour, Date, Place	Summary of Events and Information	Remarks and references to Appendices
3/1/5 (Continued)	Ambulance wagons to be proceed to L/CPL under 1 Officer, to assist at Braemar Station, sent Capt FRASER & Lectin. Bearer Subdivision with wagons for this duty. Orders received to notify Duty to O.C. Braemar Station, WESTOUTRE, numbers that can be accommodated at Convalescent Depot and arrange for their transport from that place to the Depot. The Rev. I.T. KEMPSTER, Wesleyan Chaplain, arrived & reported himself for duty with No. 9 F. Ambulance. Arranged for his billetting.	SWA
6pm +15 BERTHEN	Went round horses, one suspicious case of "mange" isolated and was sent to veterinary Officer. Arranged about building an Aldershot Kitchen for use of sick of Convalescent Depot. Saw A.D.M.S., arranged that the men sent from WESTOUTRE and L/CRE for admission to the Convalescent Depot should be sent by the Ambulance wagons of 7 F.A.	SWA

WAR DIARY

INTELLIGENCE SUMMARY.

(Erase heading not required.)

Army Form C. 2118.

Hour, Date, Place	Summary of Events and Information	Remarks and references to Appendices
4.15 (Continued)	Field Ambulances and that R.C. Convalescent Depot would notify A.D.M.S. every morning of accommodation available. Afternoon went down to Dressing Station at ST JEANS CAPPEL, found things satisfactory. 3 cases, 1 for evacuation & 2 detained. Made a note of certain things required for benefit of sick there. Orders received to move N. Immediately from Chilcan to make room for Fd. Fd. 6 No. R.A. This was carried out, also the horses moved to shelter in the field behind the farm occupied by the rear of the unit. Notified from Him that Col McLOUGHLIN would return to take over command of the unit when he was relieved by Col. GEDDES at 11 pm. Went round horses with A.D.V.S. Two with mange and one lame one sent away. Notified him that to amplify 9 through hit & hurting me assumed Capt ROBERTS & Lieut WILSON with B Echelon Sent Lieut Orr left at 11 am to take over Dressing Station at WESTOUTRE and went mad returned from ST JEAN CAPPE L having handed over the Dressing Station to his F.A. Ambulance there. Lt Col. McLOUGHLIN returned about 5 pm. Stood	P.M. P.M.
6pm 5.15 BERTHEN		

WAR DIARY
INTELLIGENCE SUMMARY.
(Erase heading not required.)

Army Form C. 2118.

Hour, Date, Place	Summary of Events and Information	Remarks and references to Appendices
6 p.m. 6/15. BERTHEN.	Resumed command of the unit today. Colonel GEDDES. A.M.S. and 3rd Division called during the day and visited Convalescent Depot and the Dressing Station at MESTOUTRE.	B.S.Hodges.
6 p.m. 7/15. BERTHEN.	No more.	Lieut. Witham b.
6 p.m. 8/15. BERTHEN.	A.D.M.S. visited Trappist monastery to ascertain its suitability for use as a Convalescent Depot. Capt. FRASER proceeded on 8 days leave to ENGLAND.	2nd Lt Cpt. J. Gambie. gd.
6 p.m. 9/15. BERTHEN.	G.O.C. Cavalry 1st Corps and 3rd Division visited Convalescent Depot. 1 case of measles (3rd Siege By. R.G.A) taken in charge at Dressing Station MESTOUTRE, and passed on to Clearing Hospital, disease probably contracted at HAZEBROUCK.	gd.
6 p.m. 10/15. BERTHEN.	Jenny draught horse No19. Aldershot, which had broken loose from Horse lines was found drowned at about 5 a.m. this morning.	gd.
6 p.m. 11/15. BERTHEN.	Court of Inquiry held on death of horse referred to above. Proceedings sent to A.D.M.L 1 man posted	gd.

Army Form C. 2118.

WAR DIARY
or
INTELLIGENCE SUMMARY.
(Erase heading not required.)

Instructions regarding War Diaries and Intelligence Summaries are contained in F.S. Regs., Part II. and the Staff Manual respectively. Title pages will be prepared in manuscript.

Hour, Date, Place	Summary of Events and Information	Remarks and references to Appendices
11/5 (continued)	transferred to Royal Irish Rifles for water duties, under instructions of A.D.M.S. 2nd Divn.	S/L
12.15 6pm. BERTHEN	3 men transferred to 1st Bn. Northumberland Fusrs. and 2 to 1st Bn. Lincolnshire Regiment for water duties, under instructions of A.D.M.S. 2nd Divn.	S/L
6pm 13/5. BERTHEN	"B" Section Tent Subdivision drawn from the Dressing Station WESTOUTRE under orders of A.D.M.S. 2nd Divn.	Order attached S/L
6pm 14/5. BERTHEN	Lieut. J.A. FLEMING and 3 men proceeded to WESTOUTRE under verbal orders of A.D.M.S. to assume charge of the Bath and for other Sanitary Duties.	S/L
6pm 15/5. BERTHEN	A.D.M.S. visited this morning.	S/L
6pm 16/5. BERTHEN	Capt. A.D. FRASER returned from leave l/noct evening.	S/L
6pm 17/5. BERTHEN	No move.	S/L
6pm 18/5. BERTHEN	No 20891 Pte MACKERNESS of this unit transferred today to G.H.Q. under instructions of D.M.S. S. SALAMKIN	S/L

WAR DIARY
INTELLIGENCE SUMMARY.
(Erase heading not required.)

Army Form C. 2118.

Hour, Date, Place	Summary of Events and Information	Remarks and references to Appendices
18/5 (Continued)	of the Unit, granted 8 days leave to ENGLAND.	
6pm 19/5. BERTHEN.	A.D.M.S. 3rd Division visited today.	Sgd L
6pm 20/5. BERTHEN.	No more.	Sgd L
6pm 21/5. BERTHEN.	D.D.M.S. called and instructed Major E.H. BUSS hands to visit 27th Division daily, with a view to reducing the wastage due to sickness in that Division	Sgd L
6pm 22/5. BERTHEN	Notification received from A.D.M.S. that the small establishment at WESTOUTRE being run by the Detachment of the Unit sent there on 14th inst, would be regarded as a Branch of the Convalescent Depot at BERTHEN.	Sgd L
6pm 23/5. BERTHEN.	Capt ROBERTS, & Lt LEWIS and 4 men proceeded to the Branch Convalescent Depot, WESTOUTRE today for duty.	Sgd L
6pm 24/5. BERTHEN.	No. 4148 Pte HOPWOOD of the unit granted 8 days leave to England, no special case.	Sgd L
6pm 25/5. BERTHEN.	No more.	Sgd L

Army Form C. 2118.

WAR DIARY
or
INTELLIGENCE SUMMARY.
(Erase heading not required.)

Instructions regarding War Diaries and Intelligence Summaries are contained in F.S. Regs., Part II. and the Staff Manual respectively. Title pages will be prepared in manuscript.

Hour, Date, Place		Summary of Events and Information	Remarks and references to Appendices
6pm. 26/1/5.	BERTHEN.	S.Sgt. McCUNE of the unit granted leave of absence to England until 2nd February/15.	9a/t
6pm. 27/15.	BERTHEN.	No move.	9a/t
6pm. 28/15.	BERTHEN.	1 Corporal Lance Corporal and 29 privates arrived today (reinforcements), the unit is still 7 N.C.O's and men below Establishment.	9a/t
6pm. 29/15.	BERTHEN.	Lieut. M. AYENT R.amb.(S.R.) evacuated to No. 8 Casualty Clearing Station, BAILLEUL today, sick.	9a/t
6pm. 30/15.	BERTHEN.	D.M.S. 2nd Army visited today.	9a/t
6pm. 31/15.	BERTHEN.	No move.	9a/t
		End of January 1915.	
		A Diary relating to the Convalescent Depôt, BERTHEN, which is being worked by a section of this unit under Major W.E. HUDLESTON R.amb., is attached.	

E Shtongsley
Lt Col. R.amb.
O.C. g/t 7th Ambulance

9th Field Ambulance

Vol VII

WAR DIARY
INTELLIGENCE SUMMARY.
(Erase heading not required.)

Army Form C. 2118
9th Field Ambulance
2nd Division
February 1915

Hour, Date, Place	Summary of Events and Information	Remarks and references to Appendices
6pm 1st Feby 1915. BERTHEN.	Verbal instructions received yesterday from A.D.M.S 2nd Divn. to commence clipping the horses of the unit.	G. Shibbon Gibbons Lt Colonel OC 9th F Ambce
6pm 2/2/15. BERTHEN.	The personnel and equipment of the branch Convalescent Depot at VESTOUTRE adjusted today, so that the Personnel and Equipment now belong to one section, with the exception of Capt. ROBERTS the O.C. Col. GEDDES, and A.D.M.S. proceed on leave of absence to ENGLAND tomorrow. Major E.W. BLISS will assume command of the unit, during the period I am performing the duties of A.D.M.S.	Gen'l
6pm 3/2/15. BERTHEN.	Assumed command from Lt Col. McLOUGHLIN proceeding on temporary duty as A.D.M.S 2nd Division. Notified A.D.M.S 2nd Divn. that 15 heavy draught horses are now required to complete.	Geo Bliss Major Bambe OC 9th F Ambce
6pm 4/2/15. BERTHEN.		
6pm 5/2/15. BERTHEN.	Visited by A.D.M.S. at 10 a.m. the unit paraded ready to march off at 11 a.m. He then inspected them and noted	

WAR DIARY
INTELLIGENCE SUMMARY
(Erase heading not required.)

Army Form C. 2118.

Hour, Date, Place	Summary of Events and Information	Remarks and references to Appendices
5/7/15 (Continued)	noted certain deficiencies which steps are being taken to make good. Lieut. WILSON left for temporary duty with the "Liverpool Scottish"	GM
6/7/15 – 6pm. BERTHEN	Veterinary Officer inspected all horses of Unit & found one doubtful case of "mange", this has been isolated. A class of 12 men is being trained in "water duties". 8 General Duty men of the unit were posted for duty to various units of the 3rd Division yesterday, note instructions of about	GM
7/7/15 – 6pm. BERTHEN	A.D. and 3rd Division visited Convalescent detachment. G.O.C. wishes it run on non-alcoholic lines. Deficiency in horses not yet made up. The attention of A.D.V.S. has been called to it. A census of local heavy draught horses is being made in case they were needed to move the unit.	GM
6pm 8/7/15. BERTHEN.	A.D.M.S. called, one sick horse ? mange sent to the Mobile Veterinary Section and kept there by the O.C., Lieut MOOD left on week-end leave	GM

Forms/C. 2118/11.

Army Form C. 2118.

WAR DIARY
INTELLIGENCE SUMMARY.
(Erase heading not required.)

Instructions regarding War Diaries and Intelligence Summaries are contained in F.S. Regs., Part II. and the Staff Manual respectively. Title pages will be prepared in manuscript.

Hour, Date, Place	Summary of Events and Information	Remarks and references to Appendices
8/75 (continued)	leave to England.	Pol
6pm 9/75. BERTHEN.	Nothing of note occurred.	IM
1pm. 10/75. BERTHEN.	Lt. Col. McLOUGHLIN rejoined this evening and resumed command of the unit.	Ind
1pm. 11/75. BERTHEN.	Rejoined unit from Temporary duty as a 2nd 2nd Division. Yesterday, and resumed command.	S.S.McLoughlin Lt. Col. Cmd. O.C. 9th ? ?tre
6pm 12/75 BERTHEN	Nothing of note occurred.	
6pm 13/75 BERTHEN	Col. GEDDES, A.?.?. 2nd Division visited today.	?
6pm 14/75 BERTHEN	15 remounts received by unit today, 6 H. draught and 10 light draughts, 15 Heavy draughts were required, unit now 11 Heavy draught horses short and 11 light draught surplus, this was reported to a.?.?. 2nd Division.	? ?
6pm 15/75 BERTHEN	No. 2086 Pte C. GRIMES of the unit granted special leave to ENGLAND for 5 days.	??
6pm 16/75 BERTHEN	Nothing of note occurred.	??

Army Form C. 2118.

WAR DIARY
INTELLIGENCE SUMMARY.
(Erase heading not required.)

Instructions regarding War Diaries and Intelligence Summaries are contained in F.S. Regs., Part II. and the Staff Manual respectively. Title pages will be prepared in manuscript.

Hour, Date, Place	Summary of Events and Information	Remarks and references to Appendices
6pm 17/7/15 BERTHEN.	Nothing of note occurred.	
6pm 18/7/15 BERTHEN.	Sgt BLAND A/C and Pt. MILLARDALE both of this unit granted 6 days leave to ENGLAND. A number of NCO's and men who had previously been recommended were promoted to various acting ranks with pay (authority D.G.M.S., G.H.Q. No.7.1/48 of 17/7/15.)	GRO GRO
4pm 19/7/15 BERTHEN.	Nothing of note occurred.	
9am 20/7/15 BERTHEN.	Proceeded to H.Q. Quarters 3rd Division to assume the duties of D.A.D.M.S.(Temporarily) Command of unit taken over by Major Van BLISS R.amb.	GRO GRO
4pm 20/7/15. BERTHEN.	Took over command from Lt Col. McLOUGHLIN leaving to act as D.A.D.M.S. as a temporary measure; 1 Corporal and 13 Privates R.amb reinforcements arrived to day.	E.W. Blus Bt Col. V.ham
6pm 21/7/15. BERTHEN.	O/C 3rd Division visited Divisional Rest Detachment. Corp'l THOMPSON hamb posted to 30th Fd R.7.A. for duty today in relief of Sergt BRUGH R.amb under instructions of admin	

WAR DIARY
or
INTELLIGENCE SUMMARY.
Army Form C. 2118.

(Erase heading not required.)

Hour, Date, Place	Summary of Events and Information	Remarks and references to Appendices
6 pm 21/7/15 BERTHEN.	Lieut. J.A. FLEMING R.A.M.C. (Temp. Com'n.) proceeded last evening from Divi'l Fd. Detachment NESTOUTRE to take over medical charge of 2nd Buffs Regiment, 6th Infy. Bde. (in accordance with instructions of A.D.M.S. 2nd Divi'n). He was relieved at NESTOUTRE by Lieut. I.D. WILSON R.A.M.C. (Temp. Com'n).	Fwd
6 pm 22/7/15. BERTHEN.	Sergt BROUGH R.A.M.C. joined for duty last evening on being relieved from duty with 3rd K.R.R.	Fwd
6 pm 23/7/15. BERTHEN.	Nothing of note occurred.	Fwd
6 pm 24/7/15 BERTHEN	Major HUDLESTON and Capt. ROBERTS left on leave to England last night. Divisional Fd. Detachment inspected by A.D.M.S. Capt. FRASER took over charge of Divi'l Fd. Detachment NESTOUTRE, during leave of Capt. ROBERTS.	Fwd
6 pm 25/7/15. BERTHEN.	Nothing of note to report.	
6 pm 26/7/15 BERTHEN.	Lieut. Col. McLOUGHLIN proceeded on 8 days leave.	Fwd

Army Form C. 2118.

WAR DIARY
or
INTELLIGENCE SUMMARY.
(Erase heading not required.)

Instructions regarding War Diaries and Intelligence Summaries are contained in F.S. Regs., Part II. and the Staff Manual respectively. Title pages will be prepared in manuscript.

Hour, Date, Place	Summary of Events and Information	Remarks and references to Appendices
26/2/15 (Continued)	Still want 10 heavy draught horses to complete unit there being 10 light draught surplus which are unfit for the heavy work with the Ambulance or General Service wagons	MA
6pm 24/2/15 BERTHEN	Lieut: CONWAY, Quarter Master proceeded on 8 days leave today, no further cases of mange have occurred amongst the horses. End of February 1915.	MA
6pm 28/2/15 BERTHEN	Nothing special to note. A Diary relating to the Divisional Rest Detachment, BERTHEN, which is being worked by 'C' Section of this unit under Major M E HUDLESTON, R.a.m.b, is attached.	MA

G W Mc Nee
Lt Col R.amb.
O.C 9th Field Ambulance

Army Form C. 2118.

WAR DIARY
or
INTELLIGENCE SUMMARY.
(Erase heading not required.)

Instructions regarding War Diaries and Intelligence Summaries are contained in F.S. Regs., Part II. and the Staff Manual respectively. Title pages will be prepared in manuscript.

Hour, Date, Place	Summary of Events and Information	Remarks and references to Appendices
1st Feb BERTHEN	Thirty admitted, eighteen discharged to duty, discharged to C.C. Station nine. Visit by A.D.C. 2nd Corps and G.O.C. 3rd Division, latter proceeded a Gramophone. Two officers sent to L.A.F.E.	Mr Michelin, Maj Rowell
2.2.15	Twenty admitted, four discharged to duty, discharged C.C.S. three. One officer of Flanes to duty.	MM
3.2.15	Twenty admitted, discharged to duty to C.C. Station three. Body of Italian Baron Cornet Nov. 2nd Most Sens. Chevin, brought down to C.C. Station three.	MM
4.2.15	No admissions, discharged twenty to C.C. Station three.	MM
	Thirty three of personnel 1/9th L.N. Lancs R.C. billeted & disinfected & disinfested.	MM
5.2.15	Twenty admitted, discharged twenty eighteen, casualty C.S. four.	MM
6.2.15	Ten admitted, discharged to duty six, to Casualty Clearing Station six. An eighty bag cylin. dated m'k'd H.Q.H.Q. creative roles patients on S.F.S. drawing of attention to P.J.R.U. C.A. viz 90.Q.	Report of ammunition used & rounds sent to hq.f.
7.2.15	Twenty admitted, discharged to duty thirteen, to C.C. Station five. Visit by Lt Col W. Long R.A. acting S.D.M.S. to whom I again pointed out that Statistics were the thing I objected to & he seemed I know. On account of the sending of cases from here who after they had been under treatment for several days. Afternoon visit by G.O.C. II Corps.	MM
8.2.15	Twenty admitted, discharged to duty four to C.C. Station nine.	MM
9.2.15	Twenty admitted, discharged twenty four, to C.C. Station five.	MM
10.2.15	admitted, discharged to duty nine, to C.C. Station four.	MM

Army Form C. 2118.

WAR DIARY
or
INTELLIGENCE SUMMARY.
(Erase heading not required.)

Instructions regarding War Diaries and Intelligence Summaries are contained in F. S. Regs., Part II. and the Staff Manual respectively. Title pages will be prepared in manuscript.

Hour, Date, Place	Summary of Events and Information	Remarks and references to Appendices
11.2.15 P.O.F.G. II-5 N	Four admitted, discharged to duty two, to C.C. Station four.	Medical Arrangement
12.2.15 "	Ten admitted, discharged to duty twenty, to C.C. Station three. Inspection by ADMS, his attention drawn to cases detained of one to 5-21 days, and thanks due here.	MA
13.2.15 "	admitted, discharged to duty 10 to C.C. Station nil	MA
14.2.15 "	Ten twenty two admitted, discharged to duty ten, to C.C. Station six. OC 2 Army gone west (Rest Det:)	MA
15.2.15 "	Twenty two admitted – discharged to duty eight to C.C. Station two	MA
16.2.15 "	Twenty admitted discharged to duty twenty, to C.C. Station three Paid Carriers Francs 45/1 New arrangement to dispatch sick chrons in full Appn Plain cases between in case of a nine. Appr KT II	MA Appn II MA
17.2.15 "	Ten admitted, discharged to duty nine, to C.C.S there	
18.2.15 "	Ten admitted, discharged to duty eight to C.C.S me Discharge in this week in ADMS month arrangement upon LA CYTTE	MA
19.2.15 "	Ten admitted, discharged to duty eight, CCS fin from Battn DUDERDONY MA C.C. Station three g.k. Rt Rept Back	
20.2.15 "	Twenty admitted, twenty two duty thirteen, C.C. Station four do	MA
21.2.15 "	Twenty admitted, twenty nine, got 3 down theater	MA
22.2.15 "	Ten admitted, twenty ten, CCS fire do	MA
23.2.15 "	Ten admitted, twenty twenty three, CCS there do	MA

Army Form C. 2118.

WAR DIARY
or
INTELLIGENCE SUMMARY.
(Erase heading not required.)

Instructions regarding War Diaries and Intelligence Summaries are contained in F.S. Regs., Part II. and the Staff Manual respectively. Title pages will be prepared in manuscript.

Hour, Date, Place	Summary of Events and Information	Remarks and references to Appendices
24.2.15 BERTHEN	Major Anderston proceeded on leave.	MM.
25-2.15	20 Returns of discharges to duty 1 to. CCS	
26.2.15	20 — 1 — 7 — 6 to. Cdy	
27.2.15	10 — 8 — 2 to. CCS	
28-2.15	9 — 12 — 4 to CCS	
1.3.15	22 — 18 — 2k CCS.	
	— 9 —	
	Repd. K.D.9 M.S.	
	The following are the monthly statistics of Feb/15.	
	during the month of Feb/15.	
	Number of cases admitted 420	
	Remaining no 28.2.15 — 127	
	Discharged to duty 299 = 74%	
	Discharged to Clearing Stn. 105.= 26%	
	Average stay. 8.75 days.	
	Presenting diseases. 26%	
	Effects of cold.	
	Myalgia.	
	Bronchial Catarrh.	
	A large increase in Cases of myalgia probably due to inclement weather & recent of recent Lydenham ailment age. Number of Staff from ell 10–4 sent to duty the CClr dy remain	

Army Form C. 2118.

WAR DIARY
or
INTELLIGENCE SUMMARY.
(Erase heading not required.)

Instructions regarding War Diaries and Intelligence Summaries are contained in F.S. Regs., Part II. and the Staff Manual respectively. Title pages will be prepared in manuscript.

Hour, Date, Place	Summary of Events and Information	Remarks and references to Appendices

Of the 26% sent to O.C Dtn. 2.0% were Mn smollen knew. Many cures and here lately have been under treatment at home for from 7 to 9 days.

Army Form C. 2118.

WAR DIARY
or
INTELLIGENCE SUMMARY.
(Erase heading not required.)

Instructions regarding War Diaries and Intelligence Summaries are contained in F. S. Regs., Part II. and the Staff Manual respectively. Title pages will be prepared in manuscript.

Hour, Date, Place			Summary of Events and Information		Remarks and references to Appendices
Appendix I					
1.2.15	No	Rank & Name	Unit	Disease	
	9389	Pte Hollingsworth	2 K Rifles	S.W.O	Inoculated & leave in June
	10917	Cpl Wylam	2/Rifles	S.W.O	" " 1905
	5841	Pte Scott	2/ Suffolks	P.U.O	
	9324	Pte Rotenoy	1st Gren	D.A.H	Not L.eng
	10390	Spr Wilkins	1 Rl Iron	Influenza	
	5879	Pte Clive	2 K Rifles	G.S.W	
	33628	Sgt Chesterly	11/RFA	Abscess	
	9052	Pte Kenard	2 K Rifles	Urinate	
	1052M	Pte Brown	1 Welsh	Anaemia	Influenza epi
2.2.15	7023	Dr Affeth	28 By RFA	S.W.O	Inoculated & & been away Aug 1914
	2819	Pte Mitchell	In Scott R	New Itemia	
	3325	Pte Jennins	1 Gordon	New Itemia	
3.2.15	8655	L/Cpl Barnes	1 Welsh	Influenza	
	5581	Pte Dilworth	4 R.Lurors	Neuritis	
	2390	Pte Lang	2 Lancs	Emphysema	
4.2.15	8438	Pte Thompson	2 Suffolks -	Gut.	
	11725	Sr Hart Ins	2 Lancs	Influenza	
	1016	Pte Cadman	2 Lancs	Intercan gannet Knee	
5.2.15	26.9	Pte Jermain	2 Lancs	Chromic Alcolie	Impo. for service
	2965	Pte Smith	2 Lancs	O.C.G-	"
	4929	Spr Clark	2 Suffolks	Neum Rannii	
	6257	Cpl Stewart	2 Suffolks	Debility	
	3394	Pte Ariel 7	1 Enduslyn	N.A.H	

Army Form C. 2118.

WAR DIARY
or
INTELLIGENCE SUMMARY.
(Erase heading not required.)

Instructions regarding War Diaries and Intelligence Summaries are contained in F.S. Regs., Part II. and the Staff Manual respectively. Title pages will be prepared in manuscript.

Appendix I

Hour, Date, Place	No	Rank & Name	Unit		Remarks and references to Appendices
6.2.15	2466	Pt Bristol	7.9th A.S.C	P.U.O	Inoculated 10 pm 3 dose biomial 3 years to.
6.2.15	9894	Pte Fowler	2 R.I. Dvn	P.U.O	
6.2.15	6940	Pte Cosby	Duffers	At Cal	
6.2.15	20416	Sapper Wai	(S?) R.E	Tonsilitis	
6.2.15	6955	4/pt Nixon	1 R.D.Fus.	Alcoholism Chronic	
6.2.15	6746	Pte Palmer	4th R. Dvn	LET	
7.2.15	6963	Pte Mcadams	2 Suffolks	P.U.O	Inoculated Sept/14 2 doses
7.2.15	13913	Dvr Davies	149 R.F.A	Abscess	
7.2.15	9745	Qn Rankin	4 Mdsex	P.U.O	Tonsilitis P.U.O 9 mms ago
7.2.15	3880	Pte Welan	Lui Swellick	At sceen: Ls	
7.2.15	6236	Pte Stullin	1 R.S. Fus	Piles	
7.2.15	5996	Pte Crawford	1 N. Fun	P.U.O	NOT inoculated
6.2.15	980	Pte Elcock	1 Welch	N.Y.D	hts
8.2.15	4933	4/cpt Wheeler	1 Welch	Debility	
9.2.15	92	Pte Kendrid	1 R.S. Fun	G.S.W. Upper	
9.2.15	8B4	Pte Frick	3 Worcestern	Fleming	
9.2.11	9135	Cpl McKintoch	4 Gdn Hyds	P.U.O	
9.2.15	73 M6	Pte Ellerby	2 R.IR.	P.U.O	
9.2.15	1860	Pte McGowan	4/ R. Irish	P.U.O	
10.2.15	13913	Pte Banks	2 R.D.F.	N.Y.D.	? Sub Pleurisy Shows no tubercle Strangely has been entered
10.2.15	5922	S/M Clower	1 Welch	English Spine	
10.2.15	2517	Pte Allen	2 R. Scots	P.U.O	? Tuberculosis Mdocks

WAR DIARY
or
INTELLIGENCE SUMMARY.
(Erase heading not required.)

Army Form C. 2118.

Appendix I

Date	No	Rank + Name	Unit	Disease	Remarks
11.2.15	6170	Pte Buck	1/R Irish	Piles.	Stretcher Dressing Station + Sp.R. Enteritis
11.2.15	6896	Pte Cain	4/Mddx	Debility	
11.2.15	1203	Pte Byrne	2/James	Ind. Ind.	
11.2.15	4677	Pte Kneeshin	1/Wilts	Rheum heel.	
12.2.15	12.02	Sgt White	A.P. Corps	Neurasthenia	
12.2.15	3969	Dr. Dennis	Medical	Tmta Buckram	For the Base @ Special Train.
12.2.15	533	Pte Gilholing	1/Wilts	P.U.O.	
14.2.15	8813.	Pte Payne	2/Suffolk	P.U.O.	
14.2.15	5690	L/Cpl Baker	2/Suffolk	I.C.T.	
14.2.15	9057	Pte Turner	2/Suffolk	Melaena Chronic	
14.2.15	8315	Pte Manne	2/R. Scots	Enteritis Markiti	
14.2.15	7402	Pte Clark	2/R.I.R.	Caries.	
14.2.15	16516	Sgt Triggs	1/Conn R.R.	D.T.A	
15.2.15	7306	Pte Davies	4/R Irish	True N.Y.D. Met. Wound	R.J.mr
15.2.15	6926	Pte Wills	1/Beds Regt.	Pleurisy	
15.2.15	772	Pte Jones	1/H.C.	Sprain W/Ankle	? Incfracture.
15.2.15	9355	Pte Sherwish	2/Jones	Neurasthenia	17 years etc. ? F.S.
15.2.15	7165	Pte Robinson	2/Suffolk	P.W.O.	
16.2.15	987	Pte Ellyatt	1/H.A.C.	P.W.O	Insurance 2 han/n.Dspop.
16.2.15	11599	Pte Sullen	2/James	Scabies.	
16.2.15	8736	L/Cpl Mewster	2/Suffolk	P.W.O.	Snowwell 2 hrs. Switch cp.o.
17.2.15	10266	Pte Gerry	1/Wilts	P.W.O.	
17.2.15	615)	Pte Jansen	2/R.I.R.	G.S.W.Leg	Snowwell blew veins.
17.2.15	10881	Pte Keene	1/Wilts	Pleurisy	Dulaceous

Army Form C. 2118.

WAR DIARY
or
INTELLIGENCE SUMMARY.
(Erase heading not required.)

Appx I

Hour, Date, Place	Summary of Events and Information			Remarks and references to Appendices
18.2.15	10699	Pte Dobrinson	4 R Suss	Myalgia
19.2.15	2119	Pte Curle	1st Scottish	Tonsilitis
19.2.15	4275	Pte Berry	21 Robert	Piles (to medical)
19.2.15	3921	Pte Storing	4 R Suss	Piles
19.2.15	8422	B.S. Mjr Scott	110.13th A.C.	D.A.H.
19.2.15	14922	Pte Champbrell	21 R.Sc.G.	P.U.O. (mental case)
20.2.15	6186	Gunr Fish	y Wilts	D.A.H.
20.2.15	6959	Pte Everett	H Middx	P.U.O.
20.2.15	26534	Pte Emmes	3 Lanes	Wounds 1st twenty muscles
21.2.15	9172	Pte Mo/in	3 Wrrences	Myalgia Agony Ant Septi
21.2.15	6300	Pte Sharpe	2 Lanes	As Cal ages
21.2.15	1504	Saj Bonis	56 Coy R.E.	Gastritis Duodenitis
21.2.15	9676	Pte Kelsey	Antrim	Fistula in Ano
22.2.15	36444	Pte Bootiern	4 R Suss	I.D.H age 43
22.2.15	72206	4 Cpl Synington	Robert	P.U.O. Inoculated tent /4 normal
22.2.15	11969	Pte Aruster	1 Wells	Myalgia where S/h
22.2.15	10445	Pte Delwins	1 Wells	Effects pains
22.2.15	9331	Pte Race	4 Suffolk	G.S.W. left forearm X ray
23.2.15	8941	Pte Murphy	2 Rr R	Myalgia age 42
23.2.15	7312	Gnr Clark	128th RFA	I.C.T
23.2.15	3486	Pte Rood	2 R Scot	Sprain left knee Contusion head of 844

Army Form C. 2118.

WAR DIARY
or
INTELLIGENCE SUMMARY.
(Erase heading not required.)

Appendix I

Hour, Date, Place	Summary of Events and Information	Remarks and references to Appendices
24.2.15	5786 Pte Chetland	
25.2.15	14578 Allsworth	2 Suffolk Regt — P.U.O.
25.2.15	10030 Lcpl Hammett	4 Middx — P.U.O.
25.2.15	65-61 Pte Pring	1/Wilts — P.U.O.
25.2.15	7539 Lcpl Davis	1/Wilts — scabies
25.2.15	18740 Cpl Draper	1/Devon — debility
25.2.15	3615 Pte Smith	2 6ty R.G. — Pleurisy
26.2.15	5.900 Pte hrl Rustor	2/D.of Cor. Lght I. — Synovitis Mhee
26.2.15	5.914 Pte Nicholas	1/Gordon Hghs — Bed (Innertube)
27.2.15	8912 Pte Cullen	2 Suffolk Regt — P.U.O
27.2.15	9878 Pte Whittle	2" — P.U.O. (Annrie)
27.2.15	7531 Pte Petrie	— — sciatica
27.2.15	8264 Lcpl Gillum	2 N.S. Fusiliers — to H.T.
28.2.15	9392 Sgt Clements	2 S/Lancs Regt — Pleurisy J Saffrom
28.2.15	6 blunt Cpl Emin	2 Ry Scots — Syphilis
		107 Bn Ly Wren — S.E. former

Inv both thros not Amnon Effect GSW

Hd. Qrs. 3 Division   Copy.
                      2/12/69.

"In the event of a sudden move of the Division.

The following will be the arrangements as regards the removal of patients in Convalescent Depôts at LOCRE & BERTHEN.

(a) Such men as can walk will be marched to BAILLEUL under an officer detailed by O.C. Field Ambulance and handed over to Casualty Clearing Station, BAILLEUL.

(b) The O.C. Field Ambulance will at once wire to Casualty Clearing Station BAILLEUL to notify the number of cases being evacuated.

(c) The A.D.M.S. 3rd Division will wire to D.mg.S 2nd Army and ask for assistance of Motor Ambulance Convoy to remove patients unable to march.

(d) The Divisional Supply Column will, if it can be done before 9 a.m. be sent to LOCRE to pick men up and take them to BAILLEUL.

(e) The Empty Supply wagons of train if after noon will be called upon to assist in removal of patients and take them to BAILLEUL.

As regards (d) & (e) these will be done providing the "feeding" of the troops does not render it impossible."

Copy   Appendix 11

A.D.M.S.
3rd Division

The G.O.C. directs that in the event of the Division advancing, all stores belonging to or in connection with the Convalescent Homes at LOCRE & BERTHEN are to be collected at BERTHEN and stored there.

Two men are to be left in charge and these should be selected from older soldiers not fitted for marching who may at the time be at the home.

Rations for 21 days should be left with these men.

(sd) Lt Colonel
9-2-15   A.A. & Q.M.G. 3rd Divn

121/48/1

Aust.

121/48/1
March 1915

9th Field Ambulance

Vol VIII

Army Form C. 2118.

WAR DIARY
of 9th Field Ambulance
INTELLIGENCE SUMMARY
(Erase heading not required.)

March 1915

Hour, Date, Place	Summary of Events and Information	Remarks and references to Appendices
6pm 1/3/5 BERTHEN	Two sergeants having been sent away, unit now 4 NCO's short (3 sergeants), no word of arrival of N.C.O. horses yet. Horses and men being regularly exercised, and health good amongst the men.	Stokliv #Lt. Col. F. Ramell OC 9th Field Ambce
6pm 2/3/5 BERTHEN	Nothing of note to report.	
6pm 3/3/5 BERTHEN	The Revd FRANCIS E. SCOTT, Chaplain has joined from 85th Field Ambulance for duty with 3rd Division, accompanied by 1 servant and 1 riding horse. 1 heavy draught horse died of natural causes last evening. Court of Enquiry held.	
4pm 4/3/5 BERTHEN	Lieut. Col. W.E. HUDLESTON and Capt. F.E. ROBERTS returned from leave to England. Lieut. Col. E.W. BLISS proceeds on S/day leave today. Lt. Col. HUDLESTON assumes command of the unit from today.	Sd.

Hour, Date, Place	Summary of Events and Information	Remarks and references to Appendices
6pm 5/3/15 BERTHEN	Resumed command (temporarily) of unit vice Lt Col E.W. Bliss who proceeded on leave to England. Rev. E.W. Campbell Church of England Chaplain left unit yesterday for attachment to 24th Field Ambulance. Major Watts hand was transferred to 24th Field Ambulance for duty today.	W M Withycombe D/Lt Col Comdg
6pm 6/3/15 BERTHEN	3 men of unit were disposed of today for the offence of "improperly posting their private letters."	WM
6pm 7/3/15 BERTHEN	2nd Lieut A.D. CARBERY hand proceeded today to Royal Irish Rifles for duty in relief of 2nd Lieut L. Elkington hand who rejoined this unit on being relieved, and was posted to "C" Section.	WM
9am 8/3/15 BERTHEN	Lt. Col. G.S. McLoughlin CMG DSO returned from leave and resumed command of the Unit.	G S McLoughlin Lt Col Comdg

Army Form C. 2118.

WAR DIARY
INTELLIGENCE SUMMARY
(Erase heading not required.)

Instructions regarding War Diaries and Intelligence Summaries are contained in F.S. Regs., Part II. and the Staff Manual respectively. Title pages will be prepared in manuscript.

Hour, Date, Place	Summary of Events and Information	Remarks and references to Appendices
6pm 8/3/15 BERTHEN.	Resumed command of Unit on return from leave.	Lt Colonel OC Field Ambce
6pm 9/3/15 BERTHEN.	Nothing of note to record.	Nil
6pm 10/3/15 BERTHEN.	Under instructions from ADMS 2nd Division. Lt Colonel W.E. HUDLESTON R.A.M.C. left today for BAILLEUL to assume command (temporarily) of 5th Field Ambulance, being relieved by Captain F.E. ROBERTS R.A.M.C. as OC Divisional Rest Detachment, BERTHEN.	Nil
6pm 11/3/15 BERTHEN.	6 men R.A.M.C. (reinforcements) joined unit today from Base. No BASE Camp proceeded today to 2nd Divisional Train for duty ride instructions of ADMS 2nd Division. Unit now 3 NCOs deficient and 2 privates surplus to establishment. Establishment of NCOs will be made up by temporary promotions locally.	Nil
6pm 12/3/15 BERTHEN.	Nothing of note to record.	Nil

WAR DIARY
INTELLIGENCE SUMMARY.
(Erase heading not required.)

Army Form C. 2118.

Instructions regarding War Diaries and Intelligence
Summaries are contained in F.S. Regs., Part II.
and the Staff Manual respectively. Title pages
will be prepared in manuscript.

Hour, Date, Place	Summary of Events and Information	Remarks and references to Appendices
6pm. 13/3/15. BERTHEN.	Message received from ADMS for a 96 Sections of Unit to move to DRANOUTRE tomorrow. Visited ADMS at Headquarters at supposed hour.	Sgd.
6pm. 14/3/15. BERTHEN.	Message received from ADMS notifying that move ordered yesterday was "off". Unit to stand fast till further orders.	Sgd.
6pm. 15/3/15. BERTHEN.	Visited by ADMS, who also inspected Divisional Rest Detachment, BERTHEN.	Sgd.
6pm. 16/3/15. BERTHEN.	Message received from ADMS at 11 am. ordering the move referred to on 13th (less detachment at WESTOUTRE), to take place tomorrow. Another message received from ADMS at 2-30pm in which move was postponed.	Sgd.
6pm. 17/3/15. BERTHEN.	Nothing of note to record.	Sgd.
6pm. 18/3/15. BERTHEN.	Nothing of note to record.	Sgd.
6pm. 19/3/15. BERTHEN.	Nothing of note to record.	Sgd.

WAR DIARY
INTELLIGENCE SUMMARY
(Erase heading not required.)

Army Form C. 2118.

Hour, Date, Place	Summary of Events and Information	Remarks and references to Appendices
4pm. 20/5. BERTHEN.	Nothing of note to report.	April
6pm. 21/5. BERTHEN.	Visited Divisional Head Quarters to interview A.D.M.S. relative to proposed move of the unit to DOESCHEPE, tomorrow.	April
4pm. 22/5. DOESCHEPE BERTHEN	Wire received from A.D.M.S. 2nd Division at 8.45 p.m. last evening approving of move of unit to DOESCHEPE. Unit paraded and marched off at 11 a.m.; men temporarily billetted in Girls' School DOESCHEPE, the Rest Stations run by 83rd Field Ambulance will be taken over as soon as vacated by the unit. 4 men 1 amb reinforcements arrived from Base today and posted to "B" Section. Temp. Lieut A. F. COWAN. R.A.M.C. joined from 81st Field Ambulance for duty, and posted to "A" section. 668 Pte NORTON R. amb. left today for duty with No. 1 Knee Depot Medical Stores, under instructions from A.D.M.S.	April

WAR DIARY
or
INTELLIGENCE SUMMARY.

(Erase heading not required.)

Army Form C. 2118.

Hour, Date, Place	Summary of Events and Information	Remarks and references to Appendices
6pm 23/3/15 BOESCHEPE	No.1 Rest Station taken over from 83rd Field Ambulance to be run by C/Section, having closed the Rest Detachment in the School at BERTHEN.	Sgd/-
6pm 24/3/15 BOESCHEPE	Arrangements made to take over stables and Chateau now occupied by Royal Artillery when vacated.	Sgd/-
6pm 25/3/15 BOESCHEPE.	Unit moved into new billets, and horses into new stabling.	Sgd/-
6pm 26/3/15 BOESCHEPE.	Visited by Surg. Genl. Sir A. SLOGGETT, A.M.S. DMS British Army in the field.	Sgd/-
6pm 27/3/15 BOESCHEPE.	Nothing of note to record.	Sgd/-
6pm 28/3/15 BOESCHEPE.	Under instructions from ADMS 2nd Division N.Col. F.W. BLISS hands of this unit left today to assume command of 10th Field Ambulance.	Sgd/-
6pm 29/3/15 BOESCHEPE.	Nothing of note to record.	Sgd/-
6pm 30/3/15 BOESCHEPE.	ADMS 2nd Division visited No.353 Pte A.A. SMITH.	Sgd/-

Hour, Date, Place	Summary of Events and Information	Remarks and references to Appendices
30/3/15 (Continued) BOESCHEPE.	of this unit, taken by F. & C. Martial today. Temp. Lieut. R.P. NASH R.A.M.C. having joined yesterday for duty, taken on strength and posted to A Section.	
31/3/15 BOESCHEPE	Girls' School in BOESCHEPE taken over today by B Section to accommodate overflow of sick.	Sgd/

End of March 1915

Diary relating to Divisional Rest Detachment BERTHEN worked by C Section of this unit attached.

C.J. Stonestein
Lt. Col. R.A.M.C.
O.C. 1st N.M. Field Ambulance

Army Form C. 2118.

WAR DIARY
or
INTELLIGENCE SUMMARY.
(Erase heading not required.)

Instructions regarding War Diaries and Intelligence Summaries are contained in F.S. Regs., Part II. and the Staff Manual respectively. Title pages will be prepared in manuscript.

Hour, Date, Place	Summary of Events and Information	Remarks and references to Appendices
BERTHEN / 1st March 15	Twenty admitted, to duty nine, C.C.Station three.	
2nd March	Sister admitted. Eighty four, to C.C.Station one.	
3 March	Four admitted. Twenty none, C.C.Station out.	
4 "	Six admission, Twenty from C.C.Station nil.	
5 March	Reinforcements arrived four officers & two Black R. men.	N.E. Hogbin Lieut.
6 March	Ten admissions, to duty five, C.C.Station four.	
7 March	Ten admitted, to duty eight, C.C.Station five.	
8 March	Six admission, to duty eight, C.C.Station two.	
	Forty admissions, totally Emptying, C.C.Station six. Visited by A.D.M.S. 2nd Div.	N.S.A
	Lt Wood Interview change of officers proceeding on leave to	N.S.A
	base on next change of R 1 Reptles	
9 March	Admission 2 officers 28 men to duty 1 officer 10 men to C.C.S. 2 men	
10 March	Admission 5 (?) men to duty 11 & C.C.S. 3	
11 "	Admission 10 men to duty 1 officer 15 men, & C.C.S. (?)	Capt Mark Fuller
12 "	Admission 2 officer 15 men, to duty 12 men, & C.C.S. 1 men	F.C.A.S.
13 "	Admission 15 men, to duty 15, & C.C.S. to C.C.S. 3 men	Lieut Roberts Captr. R.A.M.C.
14 "	Admission 1 officer 23 men, to duty 22 men	M.R.
15 "	Admission 11 men, to duty 15 men, & C.C.S. 1 men	M.R.
16 "	Admission 20 men, to duty 16 men, 1 officer to C.C.S. one men	M.R.
17 "	Admission (?) men, to duty (?) to C.C.S. 2 men	M.R.
18 "	Admission 15 men, (?) 16 (?) 1 (?) to C.C.S. 3 men	M.R.
19 March	Admission 11 men, to duty nine, to C.C.S. one n.c.o	M.R.
20 March	Admission 15 men, to duty fifteen, Received order to O.C. for ship men to Boulogne.	
21 March	Admission 10 men, to duty Eleven, to C.C.S. Thirty four men to Boulogne, move in the afternoon.	Hew Roberts Captain

Confidential

War Diary
9th Field Ambulance
2nd Division
Month of March 1915

12/1519/4

12/1519/4
April 1915

9th Field Ambulance

Vol IX

Army Form C. 2118.

WAR DIARY
or
INTELLIGENCE SUMMARY.

9th Field Ambulance
April 1915

(Erase heading not required.)

Instructions regarding War Diaries and Intelligence Summaries are contained in F.S. Regs., Part II. and the Staff Manual respectively. Title pages will be prepared in manuscript.

Hour, Date, Place	Summary of Events and Information	Remarks and references to Appendices
4pm 1/5. BOESCHEPE.	Nothing of note to record.	
6pm 2/5. BOESCHEPE.	Pte HAGWARD tried by F.G.C. Martial this morning. Received orders today from D.M.S. 2nd Army, through A.D.M.S. 3rd Division to report to A.D.M.S. ROUEN for command of No.9 General Hospital being relieved by Lt. Col. E.W. BLISS R.A.M.C. from 10th Field Ambulance 4th division. A.D.M.S. 3rd Division visited today.	G Skipworth Lt. Col. RAMC O.C. 9th F. Amb. Ch'l
2pm 3/5. BOESCHEPE	Departed at 3 pm in accordance with orders received on 2nd, handed over Command of unit to Capt. F.E. Roberts.	QWS A'AcHamp G.W. Blip Lt. Col. RAMC
6pm 3/5. BOESCHEPE.	Lieut-Colonel E.W. Bliss RAMC arrived from No. 10 Field Ambulance and assumed command of this unit.	Lt. Col. RAMC

WAR DIARY
INTELLIGENCE SUMMARY.

(Erase heading not required.)

Army Form C. 2118.

No. 9. Field Ambulance

Hour, Date, Place	Summary of Events and Information	Remarks and references to Appendices
6 p.m. 4/12 BOESCHEPE	Went round Divisional Rest Detachment being run by 9th Field Ambulance, now overcrowded which cannot well at present be prevented owing to other buildings not being evacuated by 82nd Fd Amb. Made some arrangements to try & increase accommodation for the present.	SWL
6 p.m. 5/12 BOESCHEPE	Inspected WESTOUTRE Divisional Rest Det. No patients are being either admitted or discharged owing to 3 cases of measles having been brought from the 91st Suffolks. These men who were contacts are isolated & being watched. Visited Divn'l Rest Det. at BERTHEN & made additional bathing arrangements. Building at BOESCHEPE occupied by 82nd Fd Amb's still occupied by that Unit. Received message from A.D.M.S. 3rd Divn, wishing to see me, went to MONT NOIR & was informed that BOESCHEPE road to the 5th Division Area & asked of when as to where Divn Rest Detachment could be formed. Suggested	SWL

WAR DIARY
INTELLIGENCE SUMMARY.
(Erase heading not required.)

Army Form C. 2118.

Hour, Date, Place	Summary of Events and Information	Remarks and references to Appendices
6 pm 5/7/15 (Continued) MONT DE CATS	Went in with A.D.M.S. to see the D.M.S. 2nd Corps & explained some recent matter being referred to 2nd Army. Lieut VC Martin RAMC found today on duty. The A.D.M.S. called in afternoon & informed me that Mr De Cats was not available but that the Matron would be trying it up again as no other accommodation could be found.	SmA
6 pm 6/7/15 BOESCHEPE		SmA
6 pm 7/7/15 BOESCHEPE	One case of Scarlet Fever, Pte Patrick "C" section 9th Ambulance occurred in No 1 Rest Detachment. Inspectors Ambulance sent for & OC Infections Hosp BAILLEUL also informed A.D.M.S. Disinfectors carried out & contacts isolated. Visited Major & informed him that only Been, Red & Listers wine was to be sold to troops. Informed him of the penalties & infringement of this order. No orders received re move. Weather continues	SmA

Army Form C. 2118.

WAR DIARY
or
INTELLIGENCE SUMMARY.
(Erase heading not required.)

No. 9 Fd Amb ct

Hour, Date, Place	Summary of Events and Information	Remarks and references to Appendices
6 pm 4/15 (Continued)	Routine very uncertain, not part of each day. Death of divi-gnl. Lieut-Cowan ordered to report to OC Hd Quarters for duty. Sergt Thunder sent as clerk to DDMS 1st Corps. A Belgian Spaun reports today for duty.	Smith
6 pm 8/15 BOESCHEPE	No sick admitted today, some discharged who had not been in contact with Scarlet fever case. Lieut Wilson came over from WESTOUTRE & reported that he had been ordered by DADMS to hand over Divisional Rest Detachment at WESTOUTRE to 23 Field Ambulance and rejoin Headqrs 9 F A at BOESCHEPE. Consequently June moved at 2.40 pm which was carried out.	Smith
6 pm 9/15 BOESCHEPE	Motor Ambulance Waggon arrived 5 Austin Cars, 1 Ford +1 Lorries. 1 Sergt, 1 Corpl 13 Men taken in strength.	Smith

WAR DIARY
INTELLIGENCE SUMMARY.
(Erase heading not required.)

Army Form C. 2118.

Hour, Date, Place	Summary of Events and Information	Remarks and references to Appendices
6 Jun 9/15 (Continued)	The D.A.D.M.S. 2nd Division came over and informed me that the Rest Detachment BOESCHERE was to be closed and 100 worst cases sent to Mt DE CATS. The contact cases to No 7 Fd Amb and all remainder less those fit for discharge to No 7 Fd Ambulance. BERTHEN to be kept open if really necessary. Destruction of kind unnecessary but to move on 12 inst. Room to be found to store remainder of Equipment of Divisional Rest Detachment after O.C. 4th Fd Ambulance has taken over all he can utilize. Arrangements for evacuation to Mt DE CATS to be made in conjunction with O.C. Casualty Clearing Hospital there.	SMS
6 Jun 10/15 BOESCHERE	Saw O.C. Casualty Clearing Station Mt DE CATS and arranged to send 100 cases there. All contact and leading to wds to No 7 Fd Ambulance separately. Remainder by Motor Ambulances to No 7 Fd Ambulance WESTOUTRE	SMS

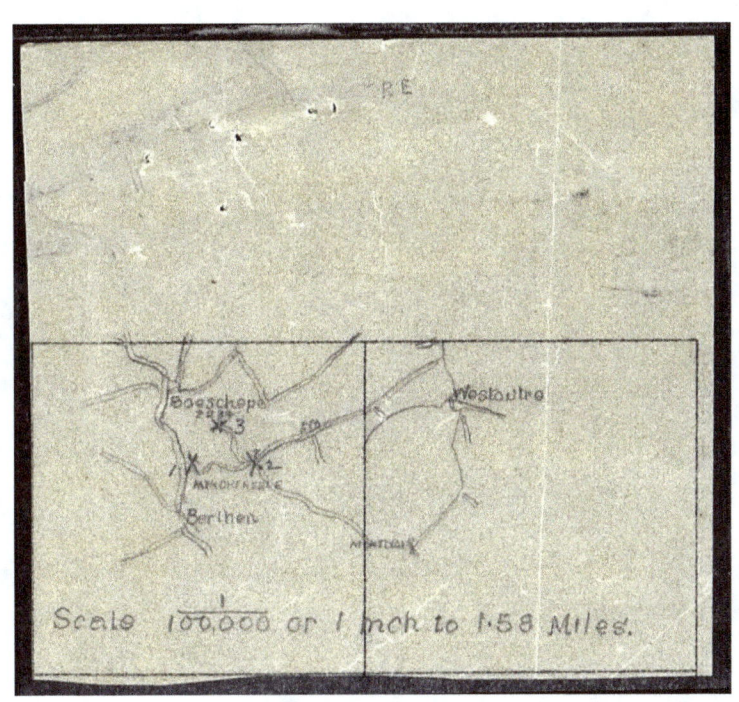

P435

Headquarters
3rd Division

O.C.
9th Field Ambulance.

Please arrange for your Field Ambulance to move from BOESCHEPE tomorrow 12th inst, and take over billets where marked X on attached tracing

11/4/15.

[signature]
Colonel A.M.S.
A.D.M.S.
3rd Division

WAR DIARY
or
INTELLIGENCE SUMMARY.
(Erase heading not required.)

Army Form C. 2118.

No 9 Fd Amb[ulance]

Hour, Date, Place	Summary of Events and Information	Remarks and references to Appendices
6 pm 10/4/15 (Continued)	No 30 Cnt Cavy Loads of Stores also sent there. At 2 pm patients all cleared from BERTHEN area. Equipment packed up & the Detachment withdrawn from there. About 9-30 pm was received to retain a M. Off[icer] there. Lieut- R.P. NASH and 1 man R.A.M.C. with 1 surgical Haversack sent back to do there before 9 am tomorrow and report to the Commandant for duty with French Motor Ambulance to be returned by them. Leave having Ambulance Wagons turned complete. returned to 3rd Divnal area.	Sd/-
6 pm 11/4/15 BOESCHEPE	Orders received at 7-15 am. to send to WESTOUTRE — BERTHEN Road to Ammunition Column for two heavy drawn horses. There were not required as established was completed yesterday. Received orders to move which to forms on the WESTOUTRE — BERTHEN and to BOESCHEPE — WESTOUTRE road, towards church.	Sd/-

(9 29 6) W 2754 100,000 8/14 H W V Forms/C. 2118/11.

WAR DIARY
INTELLIGENCE SUMMARY.
(Erase heading not required.)

Army Form C. 2118.

No-9 Fd Amb ee

Hour, Date, Place	Summary of Events and Information	Remarks and references to Appendices
6pm 11/15 (continued)	billets & made all arrangements for move. All ranks have been innoculated & either carried. Coming & Eaton Mt DESCATS, or Divisional Road Rd. WESTOUTRE, and all equipment handed over to O.C. 46th Amb Rd.	FWD
6pm. 12/15 BERTHEN-WESTOUTRE. ROAD	Handed over Billets buildings etc No 13 "Field Ambulance at ROESCHEPE and have billeted new pieces and other men in	FWD
6pm 13/15 BERTHEN-WESTOUTRE Road	A careful check of all the Equipment of the three sections has been made today with a view to disposing of surplus stores etc to lighten the wagon loads. Weather stormy & cold.	FWD
6pm 14/15 BERTHEN-WESTOUTRE ROAD	Completed sorting out of surplus Equipment & arranged for disposal of it. Rec'd received a wire from A.D.M.S. 2nd Division, who asked me to select billets at WESTOUTRE however and move my Unit there on 16th inst. Gave orders including overhauling of the Motor Ambulances	FWD

"A" Form.
Army Form C. 2121.

MESSAGES AND SIGNALS.

No. of Message _____

TO: OC 9th Field Ambulance.

Sender's Number: N766
Day of Month: 15th
AAA

Move your Field Ambulance to WESTOUTRE morning of Sixteenth AAA

From: A.D.M.S.
Place: 3rd Division
Time: 9 am

WAR DIARY
or
INTELLIGENCE SUMMARY.
(Erase heading not required.)

Army Form C. 2118.

Instructions regarding War Diaries and Intelligence Summaries are contained in F.S. Regs., Part II. and the Staff Manual respectively. Title pages will be prepared in manuscript.

No. 9 Fd Amb

Hour, Date, Place	Summary of Events and Information	Remarks and references to Appendices
6 pm 15/15 BERTHEN – WESTOUTRE ROAD	10 am parade of unit to inspect men's equipment and Gaspirit.	
	to select billets in conjunction with the Mayor.	Sd
6 pm 16/15 WESTOUTRE	Moved unit to WESTOUTRE and billeted men in a School and surrounding houses. The remainder in a farm adjoining. Received word from A.D.M.S. 3rd Division to evacuate 60 patients from Casualty Clearing Station MONT DE CATS. 6 Divisional Rest Station in the Motor Ambulances of the unit, arranged for this at 2:30 p.m.	Sd
6 pm 17/15 WESTOUTRE	A riding horse of "C" Section was badly kicked by another horse which broke its headrope and got loose last night, the wounded horse was seen by a Veterinary Officer & ordered to be shot. It was originally a light Draught horse that had been used as a riding horse. Weather fine & warmer.	Sd

WAR DIARY
INTELLIGENCE SUMMARY
(Erase heading not required.)

Army Form C. 2118.

Hour, Date, Place	Summary of Events and Information	Remarks and references to Appendices
6 pm 12/5 WESTOUTRE 9 pm do	Unit resting. About 6.30 pm a fire broke out in a billet occupied by "C" section and a few men of "A" & "B". The building was old, thatched roof, very dry and before a water hose could be piped up, the whole roof & upper floor was well alight and blazing fiercely. As soon as a water hose was got ready, all efforts were made to save the buildings on either side; this was eventually done though there was considerable damage was sustained by the building. All the owners effects were got away by our men. A court of enquiry assembles at 9 am tomorrow to enquire into the circumstances in connection with the fire & ascertain extent of damage. Also a question 2nd Division notified also notified OC 7th 46 Amb of the court as some men of his unit were billeted in the same building.	Two ₉ F d Amb GHD

Army Form C. 2118.

WAR DIARY
INTELLIGENCE SUMMARY.
(Erase heading not required.)

No. 9 Field Ambulance

Hour, Date, Place	Summary of Events and Information	Remarks and references to Appendices
6pm. 19/4/15. WESTOUTRE	Court of enquiry held and proceedings forwarded to the A.P.M. 3rd Division, he having been here to ask me to forward them to him direct, by order of G.O.C. Horses visited by Veterinary Officer who expressed a wish that the lick-up rope should be raised about 1 high so as to prevent. The horses getting galled by the feed getting over head ropes.	Pd
6pm. 20/4/15. WESTOUTRE	Visited billets of men and inspected horses of unit with O.C. of section. Our Heavy Draught horse surplus returned to the 3rd Divisional train. Having been appointed President of Sanitary Committee WESTOUTRE, ascertained what has already been done, with a view to calling first meeting.	Pd

WAR DIARY
—or—
INTELLIGENCE SUMMARY.
(Erase heading not required.)

Army Form C. 2118.

No-5 9ª Ambulance

Hour, Date, Place	Summary of Events and Information	Remarks and references to Appendices
21/4/15 6pm WESTOUTRE	Parades, fatigues, washing of kits, cars, repairs of heavy draught horses, unloaded wagons as well as unharness in being daily carried out.	Sgd.
22/4/15 6pm WESTOUTRE	Ptes Smith and Jackson came here about since 8.30pm yesterday, this has been reported to A.P.M. 2nd Division	Sgd.
23/4/15 6pm WESTOUTRE	Orders received for Rev Lieut Lynn R.C. Chaplain to proceed immediately to join 2nd Field Ambulance. Orders received to return all bumper horses	Sgd.
24/4/15 6 am WESTOUTRE	to Divisional Ammunition Column. Ptes Smith and Jackson, absentees, returned to billets this morning.	Sgd.
25/4/15 6pm WESTOUTRE	Received orders to stand-by, ready to move.	Sgd.
26/4/15 6pm WESTOUTRE	Nothing of note to record, Weather dry. Preparations— do —	Sgd.
27/4/15 6pm WESTOUTRE	Conference at A.D.M.S. Office at 3 p.m. in the	Sgd.

Army Form C. 2118.

WAR DIARY
or
INTELLIGENCE SUMMARY.
(Erase heading not required.)

No 9 Field Ambulance

Instructions regarding War Diaries and Intelligence Summaries are contained in F.S. Regs., Part II. and the Staff Manual respectively. Title pages will be prepared in manuscript.

Hour, Date, Place	Summary of Events and Information	Remarks and references to Appendices
27/4/15 6pm	Continued the test method in which to empty the Motor Ambulance wagons. A.S.C. reported that two Motor Ambulances of No8 Field Ambulance had been damaged by shell fire and asked that two of No 9 F.A. wagons could be sent up LA CLYTTE temporarily. This was done.	SMR
28/4/15 6pm WESTOUTRE	Investigated loss of two postal orders and visited APM with correspondence for advice as to possibility of a prosecution. Case being considered. Weather fine and warm. Health of men of Unit very good. Horses very fit, being exercised in wagons as well as without. Parades and route marching being carried out. Unit standing by.	SMR
29/4/15 6pm WESTOUTRE	Four reinforcements have arrived, 3 for this unit and 1 for No 7 Fd Ambulance. The Motor Ambulance	SMR

Army Form C. 2118.

WAR DIARY
or
INTELLIGENCE SUMMARY.
(Erase heading not required.)

No 9 Field Ambulance

Hour, Date, Place	Summary of Events and Information	Remarks and references to Appendices
29/4/15 6pm (continued)	Wagons sent to No 5 Fd Ambulance have not yet been returned.	SA.
30/4/15 6pm WESTOUTRE	Received instructions to send all the Motor Ambulance Wagons to RENNINGHELST & No 15 Fd Ambulance to meet them in evacuating wounded to BAILLEUL & BOESCHEPE. Attention is being paid to all fly breeding places in the lines and around the billets, as the sudden change to warm weather is likely to prove a danger from fly breeding and carrying of infected matter. Corporal Airthorpe Rame sent to 42nd Bge R.F.A. by orders of the A.D.M.S.	M.
	End of April 1915	

E.W.Allio
Lt Colonel Rame
O.C. No 9 Fd Ambulance

12/5356

3rd Div'n

No 9 Field Ambulance

Vet X

12/5356

May 1915

51

Army Form C. 2118.

WAR DIARY
or
INTELLIGENCE SUMMARY.
(*Erase heading not required.*) No. 9 Field Ambulance. May 1915

Hour, Date, Place	Summary of Events and Information	Remarks and references to Appendices
6pm 1/5/15 WESTOUTRE	Received orders to send Motor Ambulance Wagons to remove Refugees from Estaminet BRYKERIE on RENNINGHELST – LA CLYTTE Road. On arrival they were sent back by A.D.C. 5th Division with a message that they were not wanted as Refugees had departed on foot on their own further order to send two Ambulance Wagons to Camp Commandant Motor Ambulances Wagons 2/5/15.	Snd.
6pm 2/5/15 WESTOUTRE	DICKEBUSCH at 9am 2/5/15. Request received at 11.20 to send two Motor Ambulance Wagons to No. 8 7? Ambulance to help them, departed in ten minutes, there were to remove "Grand Cases".	?
6pm 3/5/15 WESTOUTRE	Received verbal orders to hold all Motor Ambulances in readiness to proceed to huts near VLAMERTINGHE to remove aged refugees to ABEELE Station.	Snd.

WAR DIARY

INTELLIGENCE SUMMARY.

(Erase heading not required.)

Army Form C. 2118.

Hour, Date, Place	Summary of Events and Information	Remarks and references to Appendices
6 p.m. 4/5/15. Mt KOKEREELE.	One man 9th Fd Ambulance reported sick (measles) arrangements made to evacuate him to Infectious Hospital BAILLEUL, A.D.M.S. 3rd Division notified. Orders received to move unit by 3 p.m. to old billets at farms on WESTOUTRE — BERTHEN Road (Mt KOKEREELE) Unit marched at 2.15 p.m. Orders received at 3.30 p.m. & and 1 Officer and Motor Ambulance Wagon of Unit & and 3 of N? 9 Fd Ambce to huts near FLAMERTINGHE to remove refugees. On arrival there Lieut Martyn found no sign of refugees or any of the huts. They heard from some men that they thought the refugees had been removed by a Scottish Red Cross Convoy, he reported this to A.D.M.S. Lieut T.L.M. Hackett R.A.M.C. and Lieut H.I. Woodburn R.A.M.C. arrived last evening and reported for duty with this unit.	Sd

Army Form C. 2118.

WAR DIARY
INTELLIGENCE SUMMARY.
(Erase heading not required.)

Instructions regarding War Diaries and Intelligence Summaries are contained in F.S. Regs., Part II. and the Staff Manual respectively. Title pages will be prepared in manuscript.

Hour, Date, Place	Summary of Events and Information	Remarks and references to Appendices
6 pm 5/5/15 Mt KOKEREELE	Orders received from A.D.M.S. 3rd Division for our Motor Ambulance wagons to proceed to No 14 Field Ambulance RENINGHELST to assist in evacuation. Orders received from A.D.M.S. 3rd Div. for Captain FRASER Reeve to temporarily take over the duties of O.C. Sanitary Section. vice Captain SPRAWSON, placed on the sick list. One Sergeant and one Corporal arrived from BASE, reported for duty. This brings the unit up to strength.	
6 am 6/5/15 Mt KOKEREELE	Weather heavy, warm and thundery.	
6 am 7/5/15 Mt KOKEREELE	Orders received at 10=30 am to send all available Motor Ambulance wagons to RENINGHELST to meet 14th Field Ambulance. Orders received last night for Lieut Colonel BLISS and Captain ROBERTS to be respectively president and a member of a F.G.C Martial at WESTOUTRE at 10 am today. Lieut Hackett Reeve sent to join 1st Gordons	

WAR DIARY

INTELLIGENCE SUMMARY.

(Erase heading not required.)

Army Form C. 2118.

Hour, Date, Place	Summary of Events and Information	Remarks and references to Appendices
6 p.m. 4/5/15 (Continued)	Highlanders for duty. One hour "Manage" sent to the Mobile Veterinary Section, by order of A.D.V.S.	Ford.
6 p.m. 8/5/15. Mt KOKEREELE	Motor Ambulance Wagons returned with the 21st Field Ambulance by order of OC. that Unit who informed me he was not going and attaching them to his Unit. I informed the ADMS 2nd Division and asked if this was by his order, he replied "No" and asked that it be cancelled.	Sent.
6 p.m. 9/5/15 Mt KOKEREELE	Orders received for Lieut R.P. Nash to rejoin Unit from Lunch Mortar School, on being relieved by Lieut. Liebington. Lieut R.P. Nash to be attached to Captain A.D. Fraser, OC Sanitary Section, for three days, after which he is to take over Command, and Captain A.D. Fraser is to rejoin 9th Field Ambulance.	Sent.

Army Form C. 2118.

WAR DIARY
INTELLIGENCE SUMMARY.
(Erase heading not required.)

Instructions regarding War Diaries and Intelligence Summaries are contained in F.S. Regs., Part II. and the Staff Manual respectively. Title pages will be prepared in manuscript.

Hour, Date, Place	Summary of Events and Information	Remarks and references to Appendices
6pm 10/5/15. Mt KOKEREELE	Nothing to record	
6pm 11/5/15. Mt KOKEREELE	Cars returned from 14th Field Ambulance. Officer in Charge Motor Transport directs that one Car at a time is to be sent to him for overhauling, notification also received that in future only Sitting patients are to be carried, sitting, in the "Austin" cars.	SWS
4pm 12/5/15 Mt KOKEREELE	The water Cart of "B" Section whilst leaving, brought over rough ground was overturned, the spokes of the off In wheel and various other parts of Cart badly damaged. Capt: FRASER. R.A.M.C. returned to unit after temporarily carrying out the duties of O.C. Sanitary Section WESTOUTRE.	SWS
6pm 13/5/15 Mt KOKEREELE	Ordered to send all Motor Ambulances except Ford to assist No 7 F.A. Andrews in Evacuation. Weather cold & raining hard	Sord

Form/C. 2118/11.

Army Form C. 2118.

WAR DIARY
or
INTELLIGENCE SUMMARY.
(Erase heading not required.)

Instructions regarding War Diaries and Intelligence Summaries are contained in F. S. Regs., Part II. and the Staff Manual respectively. Title pages will be prepared in manuscript.

Hour, Date, Place	Summary of Events and Information	Remarks and references to Appendices
6pm 14/5/15 M? KOKEREELE	Orders received to detail an Officer to take over temporary duty as M.O. 3rd Division from. Lieut VC Manly Rowe detailed for this duty. All the Motor Ambulances have now been overhauled at the Workshops at WESTOUTRE.	S.A. S.A. S.A.
6pm 15/5/15 M? KOKEREELE	Weather dry.	
6pm 16/5/15 M? KOKEREELE.	Nothing special to note. Light rain, warm. Lieut J.G. Woodburn Rowe resigned from temporary duty with 1st Royal Scots Fusiliers.	S.A.
6pm 18/5/15. M? KOKEREELE	Orders received verbally from D.A.D.M.S. to send a Motor Ambulance Wagon daily at 9.15 to MONASTRY – MONT-DES-CATS to remove men who have reported to LA CLYTTE to report there sick. Orders received at 5.30 p.m. to send 2 Motor Ambulances to a point in square 26(3) 40,000, to remove a party to BERTHEN, and to take the same party from BERTHEN on the return journey at 3 p.m.	S.A.

WAR DIARY
or
INTELLIGENCE SUMMARY.
(Erase heading not required.)

Army Form C. 2118.

Hour, Date, Place	Summary of Events and Information	Remarks and references to Appendices
6 p.m. 19/5/15 Mt KOKEREELE	Orders received to send 5 Motor Ambulance wagons to the 7 Field Ambulance	Sent
6 p.m. 20/5/15 Mt KOKEREELE	Lt Connally Kearny R.A.M.C. Mont-De-Cats at 10-30 am. Field Gen Court Martial ordered to assemble at 10 am at WESTOUTRE for trial of No 9941 Private T.J. HOLMES R.A.M.C.	Sent
6 p.m. 21/5/15 Mt KOKEREELE	In accordance with orders received, Lieut VC MARTYN R.A.M.C. proceeded to G.H.Q. to be interviewed by D.G.M.S. re commission. Lieut Glynn R.A.M.C. reported from 5th Division for temporary duty with this Ambulance.	Sent
6 p.m. 22/5/15 Mt KOKEREELE	8 days leave granted to Capt F.E.ROBERTS, & proceed to England on private affairs. F.G.C.M. proceedings received back in case of Pte HOLMES for promulgation	Sent
6 p.m. 23/5/15 Mt KOKEREELE	Sentence of 6 months H.L. promulgated to Pte Holmes R.A.M.C. Three Motor Ambulances sent	Sent

Army Form C. 2118.

WAR DIARY
or
INTELLIGENCE SUMMARY.
(Erase heading not required.)

Instructions regarding War Diaries and Intelligence Summaries are contained in F.S. Regs., Part II. and the Staff Manual respectively. Title pages will be prepared in manuscript.

Hour, Date, Place	Summary of Events and Information	Remarks and references to Appendices
6 p.m. 23/5 (Continued)	wagons sent to N°13 Field Ambulance on request by OC as urgent assistance was needed. Temp. Lieut. K.H.A. Kellie arrived from N°9 Gen Hospital & reported for duty, posted to "A" Section.	Scott
4 p.m. 24/5 M⁺ KOKEREELE	Ordered to send all Motor Ambulances to assist 5th Division in evacuation. They all returned on completion of duty in the evening. N° 12623 Sgt Mayo H.S. Rieff. Name ordered to proceed to N° 3 Casualty Clearing Station for duty on permanent transport, proceeded at once.	Scott
6 p.m. 25/5 M⁺ KOKEREELE	Orders received for Chaplain CAMPBELL to proceed to N° 5 Casualty Clearing Station and to be replaced by Chaplain BUCHANAN. Orders received to "stand fast" ready for a move at short notice. Lieut. E Lyon Rice ordered to N°9 General Hospital and left at 6 p.m.	M.S.

Forms/C. 2118/11.

WAR DIARY or INTELLIGENCE SUMMARY

Army Form C. 2118.

Place	Summary of Events and Information	Remarks and references to Appendices
EECKE	Orders to send 5 Motor Ambulance Wagons to WESTOUTRE to convoy Convalescents to MONT-DE-CATS, also to send Chaplain CAMPBELL to HAZEBROUCK and bring Chaplain BUCHANAN here. Unit standing fast, ready to move. Weather very warm and bright. Respirators issued to 150 men this morning, remainder being supplied as quickly as possible. Inspected all men wearing respirators this morning and they were trained to breathe through them.	Sd.
REELE	Ordered to send two Motor Ambulance Wagons to MONT-DE-CATS to clear Convalescents. Went with DADMS to a conference at POPERINGHE re future arrangement for clearing and evacuating new line. Lieutenants Wilson and Martyn, two NCOs & 6 men and 2 Motor Ambulances proceeded at 7-30 to the Asylum at YPRES to form present collecting parties, to enable them to see the various	Sd.

WAR DIARY
or
INTELLIGENCE SUMMARY.
(Erase heading not required.)

Army Form C. 2118.

Hour, Date, Place	Summary of Events and Information	Remarks and references to Appendices
27/5/15 Pop. (continued) 12	and boots. Respirators for all the unit have now been supplied, and the men are now being trained in their use.	S/d
28/5/15 10. 6 pm Mt KOKEREELE	Arranged with D.A.D.M.S. 3rd Division to send Lieut WILSON and MARTYN, 2 N.C.O., 30 men & 6 Motor Ambulance wagons to the Asylum YPRES at 8.30 p.m. to assist in collecting. This duty was carried out, one Motor Ambulance wagon being hit by shrapnel on the road. Captain FRASER detailed to proceed at 7 a.m. tomorrow in command of "C" Section, Bearer subdivision of "A" Section, medical store wagon, bearer wagon, baggage wagon & may establish water cart of "C" section & water cart of "A" section, to form an Advanced Dressing Station at the Asylum YPRES. No 2 Motor Ambulance wagon details for duty there. Lieuts WILSON & MARTYN to proceed at 9 a.m. for command of Reserve. Captain FRASER attended conference at POPERINGHE with D.A.D.M.S. 3rd Division re future arrangements.	S/d

WAR DIARY
INTELLIGENCE SUMMARY.
(Erase heading not required.)

Army Form C. 2118.

Hour, Date, Place	Summary of Events and Information	Remarks and references to Appendices
29/5/15 6 p.m. MONT KOKEREELE	Went to conference at POPERINGHE and arranged with A.D.M.S. 28th Division that 9th Field Ambulance would clear all the area in front. No 9 sending 6 Motor Ambulances. No 4 (2) and 2 each from 82nd, 85th and 86, all parading at The Asylum YPRES at 9 p.m. I went up to The Asylum at 9.30 pm and inspected the cellars and accommodation. Made various suggestions to O.C. Advanced Dressing Station (Captain FRASER) and then visited 9th Brigade Headquarters in a cellar at ECOLE DE VIENFAISANCE on the YPRES — MESSINES Road, arranged with Staff Captain to inform O.C. Cav. Dressing Station by 6 p.m. daily, number of casualties. Then visited Regimental Aid posts of 9th Brigade, grouped in a house at POTIJZE. Ambulance shelter on the way, but no damage done. Evacuation arrangements appeared satisfactory but the situation very difficult to deal with if a large number of casualties, many roads in YPRES being blocked by fallen houses. Arranged for 1 Motor Ambulance to go to POTIJZE every night at 2 am to clear last lot of wounded	SD

WAR DIARY
INTELLIGENCE SUMMARY.
(Erase heading not required.)

Army Form C. 2118.

Instructions regarding War Diaries and Intelligence Summaries are contained in F.S. Regs., Part II. and the Staff Manual respectively. Title pages will be prepared in manuscript.

Hour, Date, Place	Summary of Events and Information	Remarks and references to Appendices
30/5/15 Mt KOKEREELE	6 Cars sent to Asylum for collecting from Ad Posts at 8.30 pm. Attended conference with ADMS 25th Division at 4-30 at POPERINGHE and arranged what assistance was required from this Division. All collecting E of YPRES is now being done by 9th Field Ambulance from the three grouped Aid posts. Instructed Captain FRASER. O.C. Advanced Dressing Station respecting necessary assistance if required from "Frevink Convoy" which is only about ½ a mile away from Adv Dressing Station. Orders to move to new billets at 9 am tomorrow.	AM
31/5/15. 6 h BOESCHEPE–POPERINGHE ROAD.	Captain F.E. Rebuilt returned from 8 days leave to England. Unit paraded at 9am and marched to new billet on BOESCHEPE – POPERINGHE road, arrived there at 9-45... Men in barns. Officers + N.C.O. in tents. Lieut T.R. Fraser Rowe reported for duty with the Unit-	AM

Army Form C. 2118.

WAR DIARY
or
INTELLIGENCE SUMMARY.
(Erase heading not required.)

Instructions regarding War Diaries and Intelligence Summaries are contained in F.S. Regs., Part II. and the Staff Manual respectively. Title pages will be prepared in manuscript.

Hour, Date, Place	Summary of Events and Information	Remarks and references to Appendices
31/5/15 (continued)	Lieut- W.R. PRYM ROWE. Joined for duty from 1st Lincoln and was sent to Headquarters. I visited Advanced Dressing Station YPRES, showed O.C. what was required in the way of Returns and how they should be made out, also posted an additional Clerk there for duty. Numbers being admitted not very high last few days, as many cases as possible requiring evacuation are to be sent direct to Casualty Clearing Station BAILLEUL. The workshop unit- Mechanical transport, 1 Officer and 20 Other Ranks attached is sent to-day. End of May 1915	

Geo. Ellis
Lt-Colonel
R.A.M.C.
O.C. No 9 Field Ambulance

12/5935.

3rd Division 12/5935.

No 9 Field Ambulance
Vol XI

June 1915

Aunt

WAR DIARY
or
INTELLIGENCE SUMMARY. No 9 Field Ambulance

(Erase heading not required.)

June 1915

Army Form C. 2118.

Hour, Date, Place	Summary of Events and Information	Remarks and references to Appendices
6pm 1/6. BOESCHEPE – POPERINGHE, ROAD	Visited A.D.M.S. Office and as he had left, I left written message for A.D.M.S. with clerk re information as to how we should make out Advanced Dressing Station's returns. Saw D.A.D.M.S. in afternoon and explained these matters to him. Decided that all cases passing through our Dressing St. about be shown as admissions there and transfers to either main Dressing Station (No 9 Fd Ambulance) or Casualty Clearing Station. The water supply of the billets has given out, search being made for a further supply, it is extremely scarce in this part. Lieut- T.L. FRASER detailed for duty at Advanced Dressing Station.	fwd.
6pm 2/6. BOESCHEPE – POPERINGHE ROAD.	Eight Motor Ambulance Wagons detailed for duty brought at Advanced Dressing Station. Received a message saying heavier casualties expected. Sent remainder	fwd

WAR DIARY
or
INTELLIGENCE SUMMARY.
(Erase heading not required.)

Army Form C. 2118.

Hour, Date, Place	Summary of Events and Information	Remarks and references to Appendices
6 pm. 2.6.15. (Continued)	of Nos 8 and 7 & 9 Field Ambulance and "A" Section Bearer Sub Division. Went to Asylum YPRES & arranged for a "Dressing Room" on ground floor and accommodation there for cases when building is not being shelled. Burnt also rooms for seeing and collecting sick. Arrangements for evacuation charged, no cars now being sent to Asylum at 5 am. but the Cars sent up at 6.30 pm. wait and evacuate cases at 3-30 am to main Dressing Station. No 15/17 R.E. Holmes Rau "A" Section wounded in back. Two Motor Ambulance Wagons damaged by shell fire last night, De Ford and Talbot. 14.5 Wounded admitted during past 24 hours.	Ind.
6 pm. 3.6.15. BOESCHEPE – POPERINGHE ROAD.	Received information from A.D.M.S. that the unit would move the following day, vacated new billets. Detailed 8 Motor Ambulances for duty at night collecting. Orders received 7 pm to move at 9.0 am tomorrow, parade ordered for 8.45 am.	Ind.

WAR DIARY

INTELLIGENCE SUMMARY.

(Erase heading not required.)

Army Form C. 2118.

Hour, Date, Place	Summary of Events and Information	Remarks and references to Appendices
6 p.m. 4/10 BOESCHEPE-POPERINGHE Road.	Unit marched at 9.0.a.m. to BELGIUM, Sheet 27 U 40.00. 2.30(c) then put on trams, Officers and N.C.O. in tents. Difficult to get water in this area, wells are shallow and soon run dry — water very questionable, all water for unit put strained, then "Lime". Visited Advanced Dressing Station YPRES, found arrangements satisfactory there, but a need for more wheeled stretchers for clearing the lower segment of the line here by troops, and one collecting from, 1¼ miles of carry over exposed position before cars can be got to. Motor Ambulance Wagons. Instructed Captain FRASER to apply to 9th Brigade to get a large wheel hole in the road repaired, as it obstructs and makes the road dangerous. 64 Wounded Admitted during past 24 hours.	S/d

WAR DIARY
INTELLIGENCE SUMMARY.
(Erase heading not required.)

Army Form C. 2118.

Hour, Date, Place	Summary of Events and Information	Remarks and references to Appendices
6 p.m. 5/7/15. BOESCHEPE - POPERINGHE Road.	Visited A.D.M.S. 3rd Division and asked that 12 McCormack wheeled stretchers might be asked for as they are urgently needed for clearing from aid posts in S. sector of line back to Motor Ambulance Wagons. Also asked that section of No 5 Motor Ambulance Convoy could be stationed near billets as a convenient place for getting them quickly in case of a large number of casualties more than could be dealt with by Field Ambulance Motor Wagons. Obtained 3 wheeled stretchers from 8th Field Ambulance and sent them to Advance Dressing Station. One car, Austin, sent to have side curtains fitted to improve ventilation. Whaley sent in return for temporary use. 52 wounded admitted during past 24 hours.	Sd.

WAR DIARY
INTELLIGENCE SUMMARY

Army Form C. 2118.

Hour, Date, Place	Summary of Events and Information	Remarks and references to Appendices
6 p.m. 6/3 BOESCHEPE-POPERINGHE Road	8 Motor Ambulance Wagons sent up to Advance Dressing Station, under Sergeant and 1 Corporal, at 9 p.m. for collecting. I visited Advance Dressing Station at 8.45 p.m. and inspected all arrangements. Interviewed Lieut. C.C. Douglas, RAMC, who has been attached to investigate "gassed" cases. Arranged for a supply of Absorbine Sulph: in solution to be sent to Medical Officers with regiments at once. A heavy rifle fire. No. 44470, Pte. T. Vickers, RAMB, who had only recently joined the unit was killed in action whilst acting as a bearer between the Adv.-post and Motor Ambulance Wagons. Gunshot wound of chest (penetrating). Weather hot. 38 wounded admitted during past 24 hours.	Sd.

WAR DIARY
INTELLIGENCE SUMMARY
(Erase heading not required.)

Army Form C. 2118.

Instructions regarding War Diaries and Intelligence Summaries are contained in F.S. Regs., Part II. and the Staff Manual respectively. Title pages will be prepared in manuscript.

Hour, Date, Place	Summary of Events and Information	Remarks and references to Appendices
6 p.m. 7/7/15. BOESCHEPE-POPERINGHE Road	Visited D.M.S., Surgeon-General O'Donnell, B.H.Q. Explained the difficulty about water-supply in this area, also the need for more wheeled stretchers urgently. He promised to wire for the latter urgently. Desired 2 old pattern wheeled stretchers from A.D.M.A. Transport Yard, and arranged that we should keep the Halsley car on loan till the wheels arrived to fit to the Austin car now out of action. Austin wheels not satisfactory; break easily from road shocks. 48 wounded admitted during past 24 hours.	SM
6 p.m. 8/7/15. BOESCHEPE-POPERINGHE Road	Visited Advanced Dressing Station at night and sent up 2 more wheeled stretchers for use in collecting from adv. posts. 1 Officer (Lieut Travers R.A.M.C.), 1 Sergeant, 1 Corporal and 10 men sent at Headquarters of 8th and 9th Brigades, East of YPRES to attend to any cases other than the ones collected at night. Everything satisfactory at Advanced Dressing Station. Health of Officers and men very good. Weather very hot. A thunderstorm in the afternoon. 29 wounded during past 24 hours.	SM

Army Form C. 2118.

WAR DIARY
INTELLIGENCE SUMMARY.
(Erase heading not required.)

Instructions regarding War Diaries and Intelligence
Summaries are contained in F. S. Regs., Part II.
and the Staff Manual respectively. Title pages
will be prepared in manuscript.

Hour, Date, Place	Summary of Events and Information	Remarks and references to Appendices
6. P.M. 9/15 BOESCHEPE – POPERINGHE Road.	Weather thundery. Some rain. Collection of wounded acting satisfactorily but more wheeled stretchers would be an advantage, more especially if the whole were on a folding frame free of carriage in Motor Ambulance Wagons. Pte Nelson, A.S.C. (M.T.) joined for duty from Base. Great difficulty experienced in obtaining satisfactory water supply. 28 wounded during past 24 hours.	C.D.
6. P.M. 10/15 BOESCHEPE – POPERINGHE Road.	Much difficulty experienced over supply of palatable water. The amount of lime necessary to provide a margin of safety makes water taste obviously. Now arranged to clear with alum and boil instead of using lime. Visited Asylum and found all arrangements proceeding satisfactorily. 33 wounded during the past 24 hours.	N.D.

WAR DIARY
INTELLIGENCE SUMMARY.
(Erase heading not required.)

Army Form C. 2118.

Hour, Date, Place	Summary of Events and Information	Remarks and references to Appendices
6 p.m. 11/9 BOESCHEPE - POPERINGHE Road	Very heavy rainfall last night. Filled tools have been fitted up for steaming water, and all drinking water is being boiled for the men. 38 wounded during the past 24 hours.	Sgd.
6 p.m. 12/9 BOESCHEPE - POPERINGHE Road	Visited A.D.M.S. 3rd Division and went with him to see A.D.M.S. Northumbrian Division re portion of line to be cleared nightly by 9th Field Ambulance. Visited Advanced Dressing Station at night, and spent some hours there. Arranged with O.C. about new area to be cleared. Changed over by N.C.O's and men chiefly of "C" Section for an equivalent number from Headquarters to give the former a rest. Lieut: Fraser R.A.M.C. who has been on duty at L'ecole Eurepinienne returned to Headquarters on relief by Lieut: N.R. Pryor, R.A.M.C. 38 wounded during the past 24 hours.	Sgd.

Army Form C. 2118.

WAR DIARY
INTELLIGENCE SUMMARY.
(Erase heading not required.)

Instructions regarding War Diaries and Intelligence Summaries are contained in F. S. Regs., Part II. and the Staff Manual respectively. Title pages will be prepared in manuscript.

Hour, Date, Place	Summary of Events and Information	Remarks and references to Appendices
6 p.m. 13/15 BOESCHEPE - POPERINGHE Road.	Emergency rations inspected and found complete. Saw A.D.M.S., 3rd Division, received instructions to draw 6 Oxygen cylinders and gas bags and some to aid posts for early use in case of gassed cases coming in. 30 wounded during the past 24 hours.	FM
6 p.m. 14/15 BOESCHEPE - POPERINGHE Road	Visited Advanced Medical Stores Steenvoorde and Hazebrouck and obtained the Oxygen cylinders and bags for the division. Saw D.A.D.M.S. and informed him of this and arranged about their distribution. Visited Advanced Dressing Station at night and made various arrangements with O.C. Surgeon-General Tothorne visited the camp during my absence in the morning. 29 wounded during the past 24 hours.	FM
4 p.m 15/15 BOESCHEPE - POPERINGHE Road	Received information that an attack was to be made by the division over area held by it against the enemy's line at 4-15 night of 15th - 16th. Proceeded to YPRES Asylum with remainder of Bearer Division and all personnel except Lieut.	Sdr

(9 29 6) W 2791 100,000 8/14 H W V Forms/C. 2118/11.

WAR DIARY
INTELLIGENCE SUMMARY.
(Erase heading not required.)

Army Form C. 2118.

Hour, Date, Place	Summary of Events and Information	Remarks and references to Appendices
15/6/15 (continued)	Kellie, Superintendent, Horsed Transport and a few details. Arranged with O.C. 6th Field Ambulance to send up his bearers at 8-45 pm night of 17th – 18th. Arranged for all Divisional Motor Ambulance Wagons to be at my disposal for detaching when most needed. Arranged for 2 Officers 8th Field Ambulance to come with Bearers of that Unit, and 2 for duty at the Dressing Station, YPRES. Arranged for 1 Officer 4 th Field Ambulance, to assist with the directing of Motor Ambulance Transport. Had roads marked with directing flags to enable lightly wounded cases to find their way back to the Reformatory, YPRES, where I opened an Advanced Dressing Station under Captain Roberts, R.A.M.C. with Lieut. Martin and Lieut. Fryer, 1 Sergeant, 1 Corporal, 12 men, and 4 N.C.O.s to march back walking cases to Main Dressing Station at Asylum. Captain Fraser, R.A.M.C. who had been commanding at Dressing Station at Asylum, being unfortunately ill I had sent	

Army Form C. 2118.

WAR DIARY
or
INTELLIGENCE SUMMARY.
(Erase heading not required.)

Hour, Date, Place	Summary of Events and Information	Remarks and references to Appendices
15/6/15 (continued)	to send him back to Headquarters.	
	Detail for Dressing Station:-	
	Lieut Col. E. N. Blenn Ramls — " — } 9th Field Ambulance	
	Lieut J. A. Wilson — " — }	
	Lieut T. L. Forrest — " — }	
	Lieut J. B. Nash — " — }	
	Captain N. M. Darling — " — } 8th Field Ambulance.	
	Captain C. W. Dwyer — " — }	
	Captain J. Adams — " — } 7th Field Ambulance	
	Lieut D. Le Fan — " — }	
	Lieut C. G. Douglas — " — } Attached 9th Field Ambulance	
	Collecting:- Capt F. E. Roberts — " — } 9th Field Ambulance	
	Lieut V. C. Martyn — " — }	
	Lieut M. R. Pryn — " — }	
	Lieut W. C. Burgett — " — } 8th Field Ambulance	
	Lieut J. L. Stewart — " — }	
	Lieut W. E. Brown — " — 7th Field Ambulance	Still

WAR DIARY
INTELLIGENCE SUMMARY
(Erase heading not required.)

Army Form C. 2118.

Hour, Date, Place	Summary of Events and Information	Remarks and references to Appendices
15/6/15. (continued)	Attack was made at appointed time successfully. Cases were collected during the day steadily and by 12 noon on 16th, 5 Officers and 953 other ranks had been admitted. The collecting was done with great difficulty from a heavy enemy's fire during the day and following night. Two dressing-rooms were opened and wards and corridors of Asylum used. The whole staff worked magnificently and the wounded were passed through with the greatest care and despatch. To facilitate estimating numbers remaining on for evacuation, a system was started of having a man checking all lying and sitting cases as they came in, and keeping a grand total, whilst other men checked numbers as they passed out to be evacuated, the difference giving numbers at any time requiring evacuation. The collecting of wounded proceeded through night of 16th-17th and day of 17th, the casualties being very heavy. Still	

Army Form C. 2118.

WAR DIARY
or
INTELLIGENCE SUMMARY.
(Erase heading not required.)

Hour, Date, Place	Summary of Events and Information	Remarks and references to Appendices
15/6/15 (continued)	and the Motor Ambulance Waggons proceeding backwards and forwards through YPRES under constant shell fire. Two cars of No 9 Field Ambulance were damaged badly and put out of action by a shell knocking a wall down on top of them, and the steering gear of the 9 Field Ambulance Ford car became loose and would not set. During the period 12 noon on 16th to 12 noon 17th Officers 64 Other ranks 2177 Germans 41 were passed through. Convoys of evacuation came up periodically and cleared Officers 64 Other ranks 2140 Germans 41 in the same period	Still

WAR DIARY / INTELLIGENCE SUMMARY

Army Form C. 2118.

(Erase heading not required.)

Hour, Date, Place	Summary of Events and Information	Remarks and references to Appendices
15/6/15. (continued)	On the evening of the 15th a third larger dressing room was opened to speed up the work and the one in the cellar was not used but kept in reserve in case of shelling. On the morning of the 15th a Brigadier of the 5th Corps visited the Dressing Station and expressed himself as very greatly pleased with and astonished at the celerity with which the wounded had been collected during daylight and at night and the manner in which they had been passed through, treated, and evacuated from the Advanced Dressing Station. The A.D.M.S. 3rd Division visited Dressing Station at night and expressed himself as very satisfied with arrangements and the work which had been done. All ranks of the unit and the Officers and men who were attached from 8th and 9th Field Ambulances worked without sleep, day and night, in a magnificent manner, and still	

WAR DIARY
INTELLIGENCE SUMMARY.
(Erase heading not required.)

Army Form C. 2118.

Hour, Date, Place	Summary of Events and Information	Remarks and references to Appendices
15/6/- (continued)	although suffering greatly from lack of sleep were most devoted in their attention to the wounded. On the night of 17th–18th I heard there were still some wounded out at certain points and informed Captain Roberts. Search was made and a number brought in, but it is said there are still some out in Y wood awaiting clearing, and special arrangements are being made tonight. 3 Officers and 300 men from other units are to assist in the search. The numbers admitted for the period 12 noon 17th to 12 noon 18th are Officers 8. Other ranks 225. Germans 23. These were all evacuated except 11 Germans. Lieut. Bazett and Lieut. Stewart proceeded during the afternoon of the 18th to make a reconnaissance to try and find	

Army Form C. 2118.

WAR DIARY
INTELLIGENCE SUMMARY.
(Erase heading not required.)

Hour, Date, Place	Summary of Events and Information	Remarks and references to Appendices

15/6/15 (continued)	find out where any more wounded might be awaiting collection. This was carried out preparatory to the evening's work. At dusk all Bearers of 7th, 8th and 9th Field Ambulances were sent up and Captain Roberts met the Officers at a conference at Zoole and arranged about clearing the various areas. In Y wood one man was found and 26 who had been cleared by the Royal Scots in the morning were taken over from them. The total admissions from 12 noon 18th to 12 noon 19th were:—
	
	      Officers 6
	      Other Ranks 137
	      Germans 6
	
	Evacuations:— Officers 5
	      Other Ranks 137
	      Germans 17
		S.M.B.

Army Form C. 2118.

WAR DIARY
INTELLIGENCE SUMMARY.
(Erase heading not required.)

Instructions regarding War Diaries and Intelligence Summaries are contained in F.S. Regs., Part II. and the Staff Manual respectively. Title pages will be prepared in manuscript.

Hour, Date, Place	Summary of Events and Information	Remarks and references to Appendices
6 p.m. 19/5. BOESCHEPE - POPERINGHE Road	Handed over Dressing Station to Capt. F.E. Roberts R.A.M.C at 11.45 p.m. Orders issued to withdraw "C" section to rest as soon as possible today. Many of the Officers, N.C.O's, and men are rather exhausted from want of sleep as practically the staff has been working without sleep since 16th inst. The present arrangements are as follows:- 1 Officer, (Lieut. N.R. Pryn R.A.M.C.), 1 Sergeant, 1 Corporal and 6 men on duty at Reformatory (École). Capt. Roberts, Lieut. Wilson, Lieut. Wood, Lieut. Thompson and Lieut. Fraser, also Lieut. Douglas (who is temporarily attached) remain with A & B. Tent and Reserve Ant: Divisions. (An party at École for duty) at Main Dressing Station, Asylum. The Officers and men who were temporarily attached from 7th & 8th Field Ambulances have returned to their respective units.	Sut

Forms/C. 2118/11.

WAR DIARY
or
INTELLIGENCE SUMMARY.
(Erase heading not required.)

Army Form C. 2118.

Hour, Date, Place	Summary of Events and Information	Remarks and references to Appendices
19/6/15 (continued)	List of recommendations for awards in connection with the recent operations were forwarded to A.D.M.S., 3rd Division today. 50 wounded during the past 24 hours.	Sd.
6 p.m. 20/6/15 BOESCHEPE-POPERINGHE Road.	Visited A.D.M.S, 3rd Division in the morning. Lieut. V.C. Martyn R.A.M.C. brought down from Doering Station (Quarantined). Capt: T.L. Fraser R.A.M.C. also sick. ? Influenza. Lieut: R.H. Killie R.A.M.C. sent from Headquarters to Doering Station in relief. Supplementary list of "recommendations" sent to A.D. M.S., 3rd Division. 15 wounded during the past 24 hours.	Sd.
6 p.m. 21/6/15 BOESCHEPE-POPERINGHE Road.	D.D.M.S. 5th Corps visited Headquarters of Ambulance, also A.D.M.S, 3rd Division. Arranged with O.C. 10th Cavalry Clearing Station to take Capt: Fraser and Lieut: Martyn into his unit for observation as there is difficulty about looking after them properly. 6 new Henry Draught horses drawn, which makes establishment complete (as road list). Visited Asylum, YPRES last night and arranged necessary matters	

WAR DIARY
INTELLIGENCE SUMMARY

Army Form C. 2118.

Hour, Date, Place	Summary of Events and Information	Remarks and references to Appendices
21/7/15. (Continued)	with O.C. Advanced Dressing Station, 20 wounded during the past 24 hours.	
22/7/15 BOESCHEPE-POPERINGHE Road.	Arrangements made for an attack at 6 p.m. by 4th Infantry Brigade. Medical arrangements as follows:- All Officers of No. 9 Field Ambulance (less 2 sick) at Asylum. Each or collecting. 2 Officers and all Bearer Division of 8th Field Ambulance for collecting. Two 1 Officer for duty at Dressing Station, Asylum. All Bearers 9th Field Ambulance under Capt: Roberts Lieut: Page and sent North for collecting. The attack did not develop and the casualties were small 1 Officer and 30 Other ranks. Saw A.D.M.S. 3rd Division during the day and made final arrangements.	Ind.
23/7/15 BOESCHEPE-POPERINGHE Road.	Convoy came to Asylum at 12-30 a.m. and all cases were evacuated including three for transfer to the Field Ambulance. Returned to Headquarters at 10-30 a.m. Capt. A.D. Forsee and Temporary Lieut: V.C. Martyn R.A.M.C. transferred to No. 10	Ind.

WAR DIARY
or
INTELLIGENCE SUMMARY.
(Erase heading not required.)

Army Form C. 2118.

Hour, Date, Place	Summary of Events and Information	Remarks and references to Appendices
23/3/15. (Continued)	Casualty Clearing Station sick. Ordered to find 2 Officers for 1st Wiltshire Regt. and 2nd South Lancashire Regt. for temporary duty. Lieut: Payn sent to the former and Lieut: Ellis to the latter. This leaves the unit very short of Officers for collecting and running the Dressing Station. 38 wounded during the past 24 hours.	Sud
24/3/15. BOESCHEPE–POPERINGHE Road.	Revd Buchanan having arranged an exchange of duties with the Revd Evans (8th Field Ambulance) returned to Headquarters for a few days. Temporary Lieut: Felyer reported for temporary duty, and is posted to the Dressing Station vice Lieut: Wood to Headquarters for a few days rest. Two horses arrived back from mobile Veterinary Section. Establishment complete of horses. 16 wounded during the past 24 hours.	Sud
25/3/15 BOESCHEPE – POPERINGHE Road	Visited A.D.M.S. Received written orders to move Unit the following day to billet now occupied by	

WAR DIARY
INTELLIGENCE SUMMARY
(Erase heading not required.)

Army Form C. 2118.

Hour, Date, Place	Summary of Events and Information	Remarks and references to Appendices
25/6/15 (continued)	No. 8 Field Ambulance, and was informed that after No. 8 Field Ambulance had established their dressing station at BRANDHOEK they would send a Detachment to take over the Dressing Station at Asylum and 9th Field Ambulance would be withdrawn. Later on by a verbal message through Lt. 8 Field Ambulance the move was cancelled. Visited Asylum at night made certain dispositions with O.C. regarding the handing over of equipment on relief. Should Lt. 8th Field Ambulance round the building and explained how 9th Field Ambulance had arranged matters. 9 wounded during the past 24 hours.	SMS
26/6/15 BOESCHEPE-POPERINGHE Road	Very few wounded now being collected nightly. Tempy. Lieut. N. P. Hooge, R.A.M.C. arrived and reported for duty. He was sent to Advanced Dressing Station. Temporary Lieut. T. L. Fraser, R.A.M.C. was posted to 2 N.A.G. for duty by order of A.D.M.S., 3rd Division	

WAR DIARY
INTELLIGENCE SUMMARY
(Erase heading not required.)

Army Form C. 2118.

Hour, Date, Place	Summary of Events and Information	Remarks and references to Appendices
26/6/15 (continued)	10 wounded during the past 24 hours.	
27/6/15 BOESCHEPE-POPERINGHE Road	Temporary Lieut: N.R. Pryor, R.A.M.C. who was temporarily sent for duty with 1st Wiltshire Regt: was very severely burnt with petrol all over. He was taken to No. 10 Casualty Clearing Station. Capt: A.D. Fraser R.A.M.C. having been discharged from No. 10 Casualty Clearing Station reported for duty with the unit. Temporary Lieut: A.L. Glynn R.A.M.C. was transferred from No. 9 Field Ambulance to 1st Bn: Northumberland Fusiliers for duty.	Sgd.
28/6/15 6 p.m. BOESCHEPE-POPERINGHE Road	Temporary Lieut N.R. Pryor R.A.M.C died at 12 midnight 27th-28th as a result of shock owing on the severe burns sustained yesterday. He was buried at 4 p.m. Sheet BELGIUM 24 L 22 (d) 4-8 to the left of the road running from the BOESCHEPE-POPERINGHE road to the farm and railway. His funeral was attended by officers of 9th, 8th and y?? Field	Sgd.

WAR DIARY

INTELLIGENCE SUMMARY.

Army Form C. 2118.

(Erase heading not required.)

Instructions regarding War Diaries and Intelligence Summaries are contained in F.S. Regs., Part II. and the Staff Manual respectively. Title pages will be prepared in manuscript.

Hour, Date, Place	Summary of Events and Information	Remarks and references to Appendices
28/6/15 (continued)	Ambulances and also from No 10 Casualty Clearing Station and a party of men of 9th Field Ambulance. Handed over all surplus equipment at Asylum, YPRES to representative of 6th Field Ambulance for use in their clearing station at BRANDHOEK. Lieut. Wood ordered to return to Headquarters on relief by Lieut. Wilson. Revd. Kempster returned to Headquarters.	Ed
29/6/15 6p.m. BOESCHEPE-POPERINGHE Road.	Capt: Forrest, 1 Sgt. & 2 men proceeded on leave to England "A" Section Tent Sub-Division returned from YPRES to Headquarters.	Ed
30/6/15 6p.m. BOESCHEPE-POPERINGHE Road.	Saw D.D.M.S. 5th Corps and arranged that 9th Field Ambulance should evacuate Asylum pending new building to 4.3 Field Ambulance. This move was carried out during the afternoon, all opening at Headquarters. D.G.M.S visited the unit in the afternoon with	

WAR DIARY
INTELLIGENCE SUMMARY.
(Erase heading not required.)

Army Form C. 2118.

Hour, Date, Place	Summary of Events and Information	Remarks and references to Appendices
30/5/15 (continued)	D.G. French Medical Services, but did not make any inspection as he had already been round 9th Field Ambulance and 10th Casualty Clearing Station. The Rev.d T.M. O'Connor, R.C. Chaplain, reported for duty with the unit. End of June 1915. Diaries relating to Evening Station at Ypres by Capt: A.D. Fraser, and Capt: F.E. Roberts are appended. G W Alias Lieut. Col. A.M.S. O.C. N° 9 Field Ambulance	

Army Form C. 2118.

WAR DIARY
or
INTELLIGENCE SUMMARY.
(Erase heading not required.)

Instructions regarding War Diaries and Intelligence Summaries are contained in F.S. Regs. Part II. and the Staff Manual respectively. Title pages will be prepared in manuscript.

Hour, Date, Place	Summary of Events and Information	Remarks and references to Appendices
Asylum. YPRES. 29-6-15	In accordance with instruction received, C Section and the Bearers of A Section left Mont KOKERELLE at 7 a.m. marching via RENINGHALST & OUDERDOM. Our destination the Asylum, YPRES was reached at 10 a.m. where I took over the advanced station there from Major Montgomery Smith of 47th Ambulance. Our patients 33 stretcher, about 400 walking and a quantity of ordnance equipment was handed over. The transport in charge of Lt. J Bone Sgt R.A.M.C. arrived about 10.30 a.m. & later in the day all the horses except two for the water carts without a transport guards leaving the wagons here. Except two Ramc & 4 Stretcher Bearers will necessary medical equipment proceeded to ECOLE de BIENFAISANCE to form a collecting post there and WORMAN were collected as right from a Brigade (POLITZE) 7th Brigade (MENIN ROAD) & 83 Bar (SANCTUARY WOOD).	Ashaus Capt RAMC

Army Form C. 2118.

WAR DIARY
or
INTELLIGENCE SUMMARY.
(Erase heading not required.)

Hour, Date, Place	Summary of Events and Information	Remarks and references to Appendices
ASYLUM YPRES. 30-5-15	The collection was completed at 2am, the admission numbers 79 of whom 49 were wounded and the remainder sick. 2 died. The 4 th A.B. employed 6 cars running cross to the main Dressing Station to an Ambulance. They had completed its evacuation by 11-30am. During the day so many men were available were employed in carrying on the clearance of cellars to provide increased accommodation for patients.	
31-5-15.	Admissions 36 wounded. 1 died. Collection of sick and wounded was completed by 1am. 9 all cases had been evacuated by 11-30am.	a.s.
1-6-15.	Another 4 N.C.O.s happened during the day. In the evening personnel & cars from 18th Field Ambulance arrived (with orders to collect the POTIZE area which had now been taken over by the 18th Brigade) they were shown round the aid posts, and the cases collected were dealt with in the Dressing Station.	a.s.

WAR DIARY or INTELLIGENCE SUMMARY

Army Form C. 2118.

Hour, Date, Place	Summary of Events and Information	Remarks and references to Appendices
Asylum YPRES	Arrangements have been made by which any car returning to the Divisional Rest Stations can be conveyed from ambulance by car returning to their respective Field ambulances after having finished the nightly collection of patients from the regimental aid posts. Soon after dawn the Motor Ambulance Convoy car endeavours to Cars for the think of communication directly to Casualty Clearing Stations instead of through the Main Dressing Station, as heretofore.	Adj.
2 - 6 - 15	At No Deering a message from 8th Brigade Headqrs stated that about 50 and 100 casualties were expected from their area. Arrangements were accordingly made for the collection of an increased number of cases and a message was sent to the Motor Ambulance Convoy asking for 10-15 cars to arrive soon after midnight, to evacuate to Casualty Clearing Stations cases which had been dealt with by (Rev...) About 170 wounded were put through during the 24 hours. Evacuation was completed by 4 am. No. 1512 Pte A. Holmes (R.I Coln) was wounded near SANCTUARY WOOD whilst stretcher bearing. One Car was damaged by shrapnel — burst radiator.	Adj.

WAR DIARY or INTELLIGENCE SUMMARY

Army Form C. 2118

(Erase heading not required.)

Instructions regarding War Diaries and Intelligence Summaries are contained in F. S. Regs., Part II. and the Staff Manual respectively. Title pages will be prepared in manuscript.

Hour, Date, Place	Summary of Events and Information	Remarks and references to Appendices
Asylum YPRES 3-6-15	Went out with Collecting Cars at night and visited 8 Brigade Head quarters where I interviewed the Brigadier and arranged that an ambulance should always meet the regimental aid post between 2 & 2.30 a.m. but that it should on no account be detained later than the latter hour. In the morning I was out with the last Car and explained to Regimental M.O.'s At the ECOLE I met C/C Dickenson C who suggested that we were not working in some areas he attaches he thinks we should attack under his instruction. They would supply horse wagons to relieve the motor search. That he had done and found to work satisfactorily, except he had some difficulty was experienced in looking out Cases brought in by Car into Casualty & (Infantry) at the Ecole. Evacuated at 6 a.m. Again Collected in Conjunction with Cavalry. First had arranged nothing but of Cases at Bumping Ground. This was found to work most satisfactorily. Lieut C.G. Smythe R.A.M.C. arrived with the view of investigating the effects of Asphyxia on Cases. F	Ent./

L.C. 15

WAR DIARY
or
INTELLIGENCE SUMMARY

(Erase heading not required.)

Army Form C. 2118.

Hour, Date, Place	Summary of Events and Information	Remarks and references to Appendices
Asylum YPRES	Got permission to go to stores & E. Cosp. where to remain at Asylum heavily shelled for duration. Again collected with Cavalry. Evacuation	D.T.
5.6.15	this completed by 5.30 a.m. Motor Ambulance Convoy to now No 5 motor. F. No 4. They are to be found in a farm about midway between ABEELE and STEENVOORDE, on the road. Nothing of note during day. In A.M. Being 3 officers Rothenstein field ambulance arrived with severs and 6 cars motor to be driven round SANCTUARY WOOD area which his Division is taking over from Cavalry. Evacuation completed at 8.30 a.m. field trav. 1 Sergeant and 6 March others	
6-6-15	5 personnel at ECOLE de BIENFAISANCE. Visited Jas. of 9th Brigade Headquarters and requested collection of wounded in SANCTUARY WOOD between hour of 10.30 p.m. and 1 a.m. (not later.) W. 447. Pt. J. Dicker. Ken C. was wounded whilst working from SANCTUARY WOOD with stretcher bearer party.	D.T.

WAR DIARY
or
INTELLIGENCE SUMMARY

(Erase heading not required.)

Army Form C. 2118.

Hour, Date, Place	Summary of Events and Information	Remarks and references to Appendices
Asylum YPRES 7.6.15	A rifle bullet taken in his shoulder and must have passed through to upper portion of his torso. He died in a few minutes in spite of medical aid rendered by R. Wilson. Evacuated at 5.15 am.	D.T.
8.6.15	A severe bang-adjoining the one already occupied has been cleared & is proposed to be of medical importance and to provide accommodation for cases awaiting removal to Divisional Rest Detachment. At midnight the available car were sent to SANCTUARYWOOD area as an attack was expected to be made by a German Battalion. They returned with four cases. Evacuations completed at 5.30am. At the latter an inspection at 4.30 am. and Attended Reburial (no.H14/70 Pte J. Nichol, RAMC) in Military Cemetery ASYLUM, YPRES.	Q.T.
9.6.15	Nothing of note occurred during the day. All Cables Checked by 3am. Evacuation Completed at 5. Rev. J. O'Byrne R.C. Chaplain, 5th Div. attached R.S.R. (Brigade) is now lent whilst the Regiment is in the trenches.	Q.T.

WAR DIARY
INTELLIGENCE SUMMARY
(Erase heading not required.)

Army Form C. 2118.

Hour, Date, Place	Summary of Events and Information	Remarks and references to Appendices
Neuve Chapelle 10. 6. 15. 11. 6. 15.	Evacuated at 5.30 a.m. A quiet day. The night was very wet & dark but all our men & officers kept in until up by dawn and crashed at 6.4 a.m. D.A.D.M.S. & Corps visited the Dressing Station in the afternoon. Sent valises and Motor Carriages arrived in the evening. Effective In. not complete until 9.30 a.m. 40 J.R. Brigade kept being relieved. No account for the delay. Evacuation completed at 5.15 a.m. We had motored into 8 Cas. umfs for transport, mostly abdominal cases. It is to be feared it is not had more than one such case. These were staged in a small open shelter, which was so very much more cheerful than the cellars has it seemed. Not worth any slight extra risk of bringing them up from underground. To provide for wh cases the communication trench & a large field are cleared out.	[signature] [signature] [signature]

WAR DIARY
or
INTELLIGENCE SUMMARY

(Erase heading not required.)

Army Form C. 2118.

Instructions regarding War Diaries and Intelligence Summaries are contained in F. S. Regs., Part II. and the Staff Manual respectively. Title pages will be prepared in manuscript.

Hour, Date, Place	Summary of Events and Information	Remarks and references to Appendices
Asylum YPRES 13.6.15	About 3pm we brought in 21 wounded from the Middlesex Regt, who were filled in a neighbouring farm and had been damaged in the result of a bomb accident. Evacuation at 8.30 pm. A quiet day. In the afternoon notify the GR Brigade Medical Officer arrived having been ordered from Brigade Headquarters to find & take on the medical arrangements to an extent which it is proposed to make in the rear junction. D.M.S. intend to open without cots an from this time being 2 pm and look to MENIN ROAD. We talked out to it. Sent to inspector as definitely the hospital and tentatively becoming arranged. Evacuation completed at 5.30 am.	D.T.
14.6.15	During the day ambulances now were employed cleaning the road leading to the North of the building, and in clearing the road round the building. A motor lorry soon so made us of a motor ambulance Hopkins motor clerks formed to collect it can be utilised as a complete bench at Coates when used as a Reliance truck of case.	D.T.

WAR DIARY
or
INTELLIGENCE SUMMARY

Army Form C. 2118.

Hour, Date, Place	Summary of Events and Information	Remarks and references to Appendices
Ypres 5.6.15	If the proposed to keep the sketches (see sheet three) on the details (full similar one). Evacuate them along the corridor leading from the exit (which the motor ambulances can now come). This arrangement will do away with the labor of carrying each case up & down stairs, and will leave the main yard for receiving only; all evacuation being thrown at the Northern exit as the motors will now be able to go right round the building. Evacuated at 6 am. All men hard at work completing arrangements for increased accommodation collecting forms, bedding, cleaning large shed to be used as garage - mattresses, etc., and clearing ward for moribund cases etc.	[signature] [signature]

Army Form C. 2118.

WAR DIARY
or
INTELLIGENCE SUMMARY.
(Erase heading not required.)

Instructions regarding War Diaries and Intelligence Summaries are contained in F.S. Regs., Part II. and the Staff Manual respectively. Title pages will be prepared in manuscript.

Hour, Date, Place	Summary of Events and Information	Remarks and references to Appendices
6 P.m. ASYLUM, YPRES. 19-6-15	6 p.m. took over command of Advanced Dressing Station from Lieut Colonel Blin R.A.M.C. this morning. MR Relief	Captains of Field Ambulance
6 P.m. ASYLUM, YPRES. 20-6-15	Nothing of importance to record. Number of admissions Wounded 52. Sick 34.	
6 P.m. ASYLUM YPRES. 21-6-15	Lieut Fraser and Lieut Pryn went out collecting last night. Surgeon General 2nd Division A.M.S. with D.D.M.S. 5th Corps visited and inspected the Advanced dressing station in the morning. O.C. 9th Field Ambulance inspected in the evening. Number of admissions Wounded 14 Sick 20. MR	
6 P.m. ASYLUM YPRES. 22-6-15	Lieut Wilson and Lieut Wood went out collecting wounded last night. Number of admissions Wounded 20. Sick 30. Visited 4th Infantry Brigade re collecting of wounded for attack tonight. MR	
6 P.m. ASYLUM YPRES 23-6-15	Proceeded last night at 8.45 p.m. to ECOLE de BIENFAISANCE with Bearer division Lt. 9th F.A. and Lieuts. WOOD and PRYN. Lieut Colonel Blin R.A.M.C. arrived at 7.30 p.m. took over command. Bearers with Lieuts WOOD & PRYN in two parties carried out the collection of wounded. MR	

WAR DIARY
or
INTELLIGENCE SUMMARY.
(Erase heading not required.)

Army Form C. 2118.

Hour, Date, Place	Summary of Events and Information	Remarks and references to Appendices
6 p.m. ASYLUM YPRES. 19-6-15	Took over Command of Advanced Dressing Station from Lieut Colonel Bliss R.A.M.C. this morning	[signature] Capt R.A.M.C.
6 p.m. ASYLUM YPRES. 20-6-15	Nothing of importance to record. Number of O.R. wounded 52. Sick 24.	
6 p.m. ASYLUM YPRES. 21-6-15	Lieut FRASER and Lieut PRYN, went out last night. Lieut Colonel FREBENE. A.M.S. with DDMS 5th Corps visited and inspected the Advanced Dressing Station in the morning. O.C. No 9. Field Ambulance inspected in the evening. Number of O.R. wounded 14. Sick 20.	MR
6 p.m. ASYLUM YPRES. 22-6-15	Lieut WILSON and Lieut WOOD, went out collecting wounded last night. Number of O.R. wounded 20. Sick 30. Visited 9th Infantry Brigade re collection of wounded for night attack.	MR
6 p.m. ASYLUM YPRES. 23-6-15	Proceeded last night at 8.45 p.m. to Écurg-de-Bienfaisance with Rhan and Lieut WOOD and PRYN. R.A.M.C. arrived at 7.30 p.m. took over command Bearers with Lieuts WOOD & PRYN in turn parties carried out the collection of wounded	MR

WAR DIARY
or
INTELLIGENCE SUMMARY.

(Erase heading not required.)

Army Form C. 2118.

Hour, Date, Place	Summary of Events and Information	Remarks and references to Appendices
	Lieut BAZETT. with Bearers & No 8 Field Ambulance were in Reserve at ECOLE de BIENFAISANCE. CAPTAIN. ROBERTS. in charge of collection with H.P.Q's at ECOLE.DI. BIENFAISANCE. Number of admissions. Wounded 38 Sick 30. D.A.D.M.S. 5th CORPS. visited Asylum at 6.a.m. MR	
6.P.M. ASYLUM. YPRES. 24-6-15	Lieut FRASER. went out with bearers collecting wounded. Number of admissions Wounded 16. Sick 29. MR	
6.P.M. ASYLUM. YPRES. 25-6-15	Lieut WILSON went out with bearers collecting wounded. Number of admissions - Wounded 19. Sick 19. Lieut: GLYNN. R.A.M.C. joins for temporary duty at A.D.Y. Dressing station. Lieut. I.WILSON. orders to return to HQ of 9th F.A. MR One wheeled stretcher was blown to atoms by a shell yesterday evening when being taken up by the Bearers. Two Motor Ambulance Wagons were damaged by the same shell. No casualties among the Personnel MR	

Army Form C. 2118.

WAR DIARY
or
INTELLIGENCE SUMMARY.
(Erase heading not required.)

Instructions regarding War Diaries and Intelligence Summaries are contained in F. S. Regs., Part II. and the Staff Manual respectively. Title pages will be prepared in manuscript.

Hour, Date, Place	Summary of Events and Information	Remarks and references to Appendices
6 p.m. 23-6-15. (Continued)	Lieut BAZETT with Bearers of No 5. Field Ambulance were in Reserve at ÉCOLE-du-BIENFAISANCE. Captain ROBERTS in charge of collection with No 3 at ÉCOLE-DU-BIENFAISANCE. Number of Admissions, Wounded 38. Sick 30. DADMS 5th Corps visited ASYLUM at 6 a.m.	MR
6 p.m. ASYLUM YPRES. 24-6-15	Lieut FRASER went out with bearers collecting wounded. Number of admissions, WOUNDED. 16. SICK 29	MR
6 p.m. ASYLUM YPRES 25-6-15	Lieut WILSON went out with bearers collecting wounded. Number of admissions WOUNDED 9. SICK 19. Lieut GLYNN RANE joined for Temporary duty at DDy Dressing Station. Lieut T.S. WILSON ordered to return to Hd Qrs 9th F.A. One wheeled stretcher was blown to atoms by a shell yesterday evening when being taken up by the Bearers. Two Motor Ambulance Wagons were damaged by the same shell. No casualties among the personnel.	MR

WAR DIARY or INTELLIGENCE SUMMARY

Army Form C. 2118.

Hour, Date, Place	Summary of Events and Information	Remarks and references to Appendices
6 p.m. 26-6-15 ASYLUM, YPRES.	The C.O. & F.A. visits are infected Advanced Dressing station last evening. Lieut WOOD accompanied by Lieut GLYNN went out collecting wounded last night. Number of admissions Wounded 10 Sick 25. Lieut. Reit. Hogg Raining reported sick & unfit for duty. JMR	
6 p.m. 27-6-15 ASYLUM, YPRES.	Lieut Fraser. R.A.M.C. proceeded by order of A.D.M.S. as M.O. of 1st H.A.C. last evening. Lieut Glynn R.A.M.C. went out collecting last night. Number of admissions Wounded 14 Sick 25.	JMR
6 p.m. 28-6-15 ASYLUM, YPRES.	Recd GLYNN ordered to proceed as M.O./o Northumberland Fusiliers left at 6.30 p.m. Lieut WOOD accompanied by Lieut Hogg R.A.M.C. went out collecting Wounded all sick & wounded collected went straight to No D.S. No. 6. Field Ambulance. Total number collected. Transferred to B. & F.A. Wounds H. Sick 4. Four sick men sent by M.A. Hu ECOLE de BIENFAISANCE was sent in by Motor Ambulance & sent to Hosp 14th Division Field Ambulance in evacuation.	

Army Form C. 2118.—

WAR DIARY
or
INTELLIGENCE SUMMARY.
(Erase heading not required.)

Instructions regarding War Diaries and Intelligence Summaries are contained in F. S. Regs., Part II. and the Staff Manual respectively. Title pages will be prepared in manuscript.

Hour, Date, Place	Summary of Events and Information	Remarks and references to Appendices
6 am 26-6-15. ASYLUM YPRES	Lt. C.O. 9th F.A. visited and inspected Advanced Dressing Station last evening. Lieut WOOD accompanied by Lieut GLYNN went out collecting wounded last night, Number of ammunition. Wounded Lieut Hogg R.A.M.C. reported here by order for duty	
6 pm 27-6-15 ASYLUM YPRES	Lieut FRASER R.A.M.C. proceeded by order of A.D.M.S. as M.O. to 1st H.A.C. last evening. Lieut GLYNN R.A.M.C. went out collecting last night. Number of ammunition. WOUNDED 14 SICK 25	MR
6 pm 28-6-15 ASYLUM YPRES.	Lieut GLYNN ordered to proceed as M.O. % Northumberland Fusiliers left at 6.30 p.m. Lieut WOOD accompanied by Lieut Hogg. R.A.M.C. went out collecting wounded all sick & wounded collected went straight to A & D.S. No 8. Field Ambulance. Total number collected. Transfers to the F.A. Wounded 4. Sick 4. Four sick were sent to No 9 F.A. The ÉCOLE de BIENFAISANCE was got in for by Little Fou cans even sent to help 14th Division Field Ambulance in evacuation	

WAR DIARY
or
INTELLIGENCE SUMMARY.

Army Form C. 2118.

Hour, Date, Place	Summary of Events and Information	Remarks and references to Appendices
Continued	Wounded. Only m. Amb. Wason was used. Colonel Nichol. D.D.M.S. 5th Corps visited the ASYLUM this afternoon.	MR
6p.m. 29-6-15. Asylum, YPRES	Lieut HOGG went out collecting last night. A. Sect. Tent sub-division by order proceeded to 9th F.A. Head Quarters yesterday afternoon. Handed over all surplus medical & surgical equipment + wheeled stretchers to no 8. F.A. Number of admissions Wounded 15. Sick 16.	MR
6p.m. 30-6-15 POPERINGHE	Lieut Wilson went out collecting wounded. No of Admissions Sick 17 Wounded 2. Received orders to hand over ASYLUM to no H3 Field AMBULANCE + return to HQ of 9th F.A. at POPERINGHE. Handed over + marched with personnel arriving at camp at 6 p.m. End of Appendix.	Lieut E Roberts Capt Peanne

Army Form C. 2118.

WAR DIARY
or
INTELLIGENCE SUMMARY.
(Erase heading not required.)

Instructions regarding War Diaries and Intelligence Summaries are contained in F.S. Regs., Part II. and the Staff Manual respectively. Title pages will be prepared in manuscript.

Hour, Date, Place	Summary of Events and Information	Remarks and references to Appendices
Continued.	3 Wounded. Only one Amb: Wagon was used. Colonel Nichol. D.D.M.S. 5th Corps visited the ASYLUM this afternoon. MR	
1 p.m. 29-6-15. ASYLUM, YPRES	Lieut HOGG went out collecting last night. A. Sect. Tent. sub-division by orders proceeded to 9th F.A. Head Quarters yesterday afternoon. Handed over all surplus medical & surgical equipment + wheeled stretchers to No 8. F. A. Number of admissions Wounded 15. Sick 16. MR	
1 p.m. 30-6-15. POPERINGHE	Lieut Wilson went out collecting Wounded half admission Sick 17 Wounded 7. Received orders to hand over ASYLUM to No 43 Field AMBULANCE + return to HQrs 9th F.A. at POPERINGHE. Handed over + marched with personnel arriving at camp at 6 p.m.	

End of APPENDIX.

Geo. E. Roberts
Capt RAMC

3/5 Binicon

121/6306

121/6306

Lo 9 Field Ambulance

Bot XII

July 15

To Gds Dn in Aug 15

WAR DIARY
INTELLIGENCE SUMMARY.
(Erase heading not required.)

Army Form C. 2118.

Instructions regarding War Diaries and Intelligence Summaries are contained in F. S. Regs., Part II. and the Staff Manual respectively. Title pages will be prepared in manuscript.

Hour, Date, Place	Summary of Events and Information	Remarks and references to Appendices
6 p.m. 1/15 BOESCHEPE-POPERINGHE Road.	Lieut: T.C. Maclyn. R.A.M.C. (T.C.) reported for duty with the unit on return from N°. 10 Casualty Clearing Station	Mullen Lieut: Col. R.A.M.C.
6 p.m. 2/15 BOESCHEPE-POPERINGHE Road.	Orders received for Rev.d Kempster (C.F.) Maclyn, A.D.C. reported for duty with 2 Troops and 1 Maltine cart and 5 Light Draught horses to proceed to 9th Cavalry Field Ambulance. 2 Drivers	M. N° 9 Field Ambulance Sgd.
6 p.m. 3/15 BOESCHEPE-POPERINGHE Road.	Lieut: J.B. Wood. R.A.M.C. (T.C.) sent to N°. 10 Casualty Clearing Station for evacuation to Millbank Hospital for operation. Rev.d Kempster. C.F. (Maclyn) and Lt. Col. Williams R.A.M.C. proceeded on leave. Capt: A.D. Fraser R.A.M.C. returned from leave.	Sgd.
6 p.m. 4/15 BOESCHEPE-POPERINGHE Road.	N°. 1278. Pte. J. Parker R.A.M.C. who should have returned from leave by midnight night of 3rd – 4th is absent. Great difficulty in getting a sufficient supply of water for drinking and that obtained is of very inferior quality. All drinking water	Sgd.

WAR DIARY
INTELLIGENCE SUMMARY
(Erase heading not required.)

Army Form C. 2118.

Instructions regarding War Diaries and Intelligence Summaries are contained in F.S. Regs., Part II. and the Staff Manual respectively. Title pages will be prepared in manuscript.

Hour, Date, Place	Summary of Events and Information	Remarks and references to Appendices
4/15 Continued	now being boiled. Weather very hot and close.	SMA.
5/15 BOESCHEPE-POPERINGHE Road	No. 1278 Pte J. Parker R.A.M.C. returned off leave, having missed his train connection in London. Lieuts: Conway, Nelson Haslyn & the Rev. R. Buchanan proceeded on leave.	SMA.
6/15 BOESCHEPE-POPERINGHE Road	Very successful athletic sports were held yesterday afternoon for the Unit. Competition in the various events was very keen. Four Motor Ambulance Wagons are being sent nightly to the YPRES salient to assist No. 8 Field Ambulance in collecting to their Dressing Station.	SMA.
7/15 BOESCHEPE-POPERINGHE Road	Visited D.G. in the Field at Headquarters to place before him an experimental pair of stretchers of the wheeled variety. Weather stormy and colder.	SMA.
8/15 BOESCHEPE-POPERINGHE Road	The Revd J. Hampster, C.F. (Wesleyan) has returned from leave to England and has been ordered to report to 9th Cavalry Field Ambulance for duty. The Chaplain of the Month	SMA.

Army Form C. 2118.

WAR DIARY
INTELLIGENCE SUMMARY.
(Erase heading not required.)

Hour, Date, Place	Summary of Events and Information	Remarks and references to Appendices
8/15 (Continued.)	Ambulance Wagons are cracking near where the cheers sweeps inwards in front.	
9/15 BOESCHEPE - POPERINGHE Road.	Lieuts. Conway, Hanlyn & Rev. Buchanan returned from leave. Rev. Kirkpatrick Wesleyan Chaplain proceeded to join 9th Cavalry Field Ambulance on Everfield Informed by O.% Workshops Unit that he has received instructions not to send Austin cars to have cracked cheers Oxy- Acetylene welded, but to plate them.	P.D. / M.
10/15 BOESCHEPE - POPERINGHE Road.	Wheeled stretcher (pattern nc) sent to St: Omer as it is contemplated to make some 20 from it for trial. A well has been sunk (shallow) at about 4' water no struck to extent of about 2' after 24 hours.	
11/15 BOESCHEPE - POPERINGHE Road.	Handed over Command of Unit preparatory to going on leave to Capt. T. B. Roberts, RamC	

Army Form C. 2118.

WAR DIARY
— or —
INTELLIGENCE SUMMARY.
(Erase heading not required.)

Instructions regarding War Diaries and Intelligence Summaries are contained in F.S. Regs., Part II. and the Staff Manual respectively. Title pages will be prepared in manuscript.

Hour, Date, Place	Summary of Events and Information	Remarks and references to Appendices
11.73 (continued)	Took over from Lieut. Col. E.M. Pilio, R.amb, who proceeded on leave. Temporary Lieut. J.L. Nelson R.amb. returned off leave.	Hw P Luts Captain R.amb
6 p.m. 12.7.15. BOESCHEPE - POPERINGHE Road.	One Driver A.S.C., two light Draught Horses, and one limbered wagon to complete establishment arrived from Advanced Horse Transport Depôt.	MR
6 p.m. 13.7.15. BOESCHEPE - POPERINGHE Road	D.A.D.M.S., 3rd Division, visited unit, and gave provisional verbal orders re move of unit to open dressing station.	MR
4 p.m. 14.7.15. BOESCHEPE - POPERINGHE Road	Orders received from A.D.M.S. to send one section to open dressing station in tents at a farm situated on the OUDERDOM - VIERSTRAAT road one mile SOUTH-EAST of OUDERDOM. "C" section, Capt. A.D. Trout R.amb. in command marched away at 3 p.m., Lieuts. Nelson, Hamlyn & Hogg also proceeding. Took 5 motor ambulances to dressing	

WAR DIARY
INTELLIGENCE SUMMARY.
(Erase heading not required.)

Army Form C. 2118.

Hour, Date, Place	Summary of Events and Information	Remarks and references to Appendices
2 6pm 14/15 continued	station at 6 p.m. and inspected site with Captain Turner. Surgeon-General R. Porter, A.M.S., visited Headquarters of Unit at about 4 p.m. Temporary Units: J. W. Frazer and J.N.d. Macpherson, R.A.M.C. joined from HAVRE. Visited dressing station at 6.30 p.m.	WR
6pm 15.13. BOESCHEPE-POPERINGHE Road.		WR
6pm 16.13. BOESCHEPE-POPERINGHE Road.	Fourteen bearers of "C" section returned to Headquarters of the unit at 5 p.m.	WR
6pm 17/15 BOESCHEPE-POPERINGHE Road	Lieut. Col. L.W. Blues, R.A.M.C. returned off leave and assumed command. Assumed command from Captain F.N. Roberts, R.A.M.C. Weather wet and cold.	Roberts Captain, R.A.M.C. Gw.A.Blues Lieut-Colonel, R.A.M.C.
6p.m. 18.13. BOESCHEPE- POPERINGHE Road	Inspected Advanced Dressing Station on OUDERDOM-VIERSTRAAT Road. Ordered out another Operating tent and directed O.C. to try and arrange for a barn or a dressing room as accommodation was insufficient. A well has been made in the billets, and 3	

WAR DIARY
INTELLIGENCE SUMMARY.
(Erase heading not required.)

Army Form C. 2118.

Instructions regarding War Diaries and Intelligence Summaries are contained in F. S. Regs., Part II. and the Staff Manual respectively. Title pages will be prepared in manuscript.

Hour, Date, Place	Summary of Events and Information	Remarks and references to Appendices
18/1/15 (continued)	fuel & water found. Quality not yet ascertained.	Std.
6 p.m. 19/1/15 BOESCHEPE-POPERINGHE Road	Lieut. J.S. Wilson R.A.M.C. returned to Headquarters of unit having been stationed at Abeemed Dressing Station by Lieut. J. M. Farrer R.A.M.C. Lieut. J.G.S. Knipharn R.A.M.C. proceeded for temporary duty to Headquarters, 56 Company R.E.	Std.
6 p.m. 20/1/15 BOESCHEPE-POPERINGHE Road	Having received information that the unit would shortly move, I visited prospective places with a view to choosing a suitable one for a Dressing Station, and also for billets. Inspected unit. Men are regularly route marching, and instructional parades are being held daily.	Std.
6 p.m. 21/1/15 BOESCHEPE-POPERINGHE Road	Received orders during the morning to move my unit on the following day but these were cancelled later as the move is postponed. Capt. F.E. Roberts and Lieut. J.S. Wilson R.A.M.C. with 12 N.C.O.s and men went up to go over the	Std.

WAR DIARY
INTELLIGENCE SUMMARY
(Erase heading not required.)

Army Form C. 2118.

Hour, Date, Place	Summary of Events and Information	Remarks and references to Appendices
21/5. (continued)	allotting area now being cleared by 5th Division. Sketch maps were made of the ground, showing roads etc. to be used.	FM
22.5. 6 p.m. BOESCHEPE-POPERINGHE Road.	Visited Dressing Station and arranged for the Clearing of area held by 4th Brigade as well as 9th Brigade. Sent 6 wheeled stretchers to Dressing Station. Visited OUDERDOM and selected billets for Officers and men. Posted Lieutenants Douglas and Kellie for duty at Dressing Station, and augmented establishment of Dressing Station by sending up remainder of "C" section bearers, and 24 bearers of "B" section.	Sid.
23/5. 6 p.m. BIESCHEPE-POPERINGHE Road.	Visited new area allotted to unit, with a view to enquiring into its possibilities. Issued orders for "B" section to march at 9 a.m. following day to site of new dressing station and establish itself there, and further orders were given to O.C. "C" section to close his dressing station at 12 noon, 24th.	

Army Form C. 2118.

WAR DIARY
INTELLIGENCE SUMMARY.
(Erase heading not required.)

Instructions regarding War Diaries and Intelligence Summaries are contained in F. S. Regs., Part II. and the Staff Manual respectively. Title pages will be prepared in manuscript.

Hour, Date, Place	Summary of Events and Information	Remarks and references to Appendices
23/5. (Continued)	and from "B" section at new site. Issued orders for Headquarters and remainder of unit to parade at 10 a.m. 24th and march to billets at OUDERDOM.	SMS
6pm 24/5. OUDERDOM	Orders moved yesterday carried out. Between 1pm and 4pm shelled intermittently in new billets at OUDERDOM. Visited dressing station during the afternoon. Orders received at night for Capt. F.E. ROBERTS, R.A.M.C. to proceed to #2 Field Ambulance and take over command from Lieut. Col. C.A. STONE. Was visited by D.A.D.M.S. during the evening who suggested looking round for billets on site not so liable to be shelled. Found a site at a small farm between POPERINGHE – OUDERDOM and POPERINGHE – RENINGHELST roads, on a cross road.	SMS
6pm 25/5. BUSSEBOOM – BOESCHEPE Road	Visited A.D.M.S. 3rd Division, and arranged to move my Headquarters to G 28(a) 2-4, also to leave 1 N.C.O. and 4	SMS

WAR DIARY

INTELLIGENCE SUMMARY.

(Erase heading not required.)

Army Form C. 2118.

Hour, Date, Place	Summary of Events and Information	Remarks and references to Appendices
25/7/15 (continued)	men at the farm at OUDERDOM, to form a collecting point for men of the 9th Brigade from which my unit will remove them to 8th Field Ambulance, also arranged with O.C. 5th Field Ambulance to send one motor ambulance waggon daily to this point at 11 a.m. to collect sick. Visited Dressing Station and found all correct. Imprest account handed over from Capt. F.G. Roberts, R.A.M.C. to Capt. A.D. Forrest, R.A.M.C. on the departure of the former to the 42nd Field Ambulance. Capt. F.G. Roberts, R.A.M.C. left the unit to the great regret of all ranks. Moved unit Headquarters to new billets, and arranged about water supply and sanitary measures there. Withdrew all possible horsed transport and spare horses from dressing station, and left 1 Ford, and 1 Austin of 9th Field Ambulance, and 3 Austin cars (attached), of 4th Field Ambulance.	SMB

Army Form C. 2118.

WAR DIARY
INTELLIGENCE SUMMARY.
(Erase heading not required.)

Instructions regarding War Diaries and Intelligence Summaries are contained in F.S. Regs., Part II. and the Staff Manual respectively. Title pages will be prepared in manuscript.

Hour, Date, Place	Summary of Events and Information	Remarks and references to Appendices
6 p.m. 26/5 BUSSEBOOM - BOESCHEPE Road.	Visited Dressing Station, found that A.P.M. 3rd Division had lodged 4 men awaiting execution there, and had had them executed against the walls of the Dressing Station. I took strong exception to this and reported it to Headquarters, 3rd Division. The Officers and N.C.O.'s R.A.M.C. of 14th Division Field Ambulances were sent here by A.D.M.S. for instruction in routine arrangements for collection and disposal of the wounded. Major A.R.C. Parsons, R.A.M.C. arrived and reported for duty with the unit, posted to Headquarters for the present and to command B Section.	Sgd.
6 p.m. 27/5 BUSSEBOOM - BOESCHEPE Road.	Inspected tunnels, dugouts etc., at Chateau Rosenthal and arranged with R.E. Officer to build a dugout near gate large enough for 4 stretcher cases and a loading party. Loading party now to be kept at chateau gate instead of front point. Visited Dressing	

WAR DIARY
INTELLIGENCE SUMMARY.
(Erase heading not required.)

Army Form C. 2118.

Hour, Date, Place	Summary of Events and Information	Remarks and references to Appendices
27/7/15. (continued)	Station, arranged for 1 ton of lime to deal with the fly nuisance, and issued orders that all the manure heaps in the farmyard must be cleared out. Visited A.D.M.S. in the afternoon at Headquarters, and arranged about evacuation from collecting post at OUDERDOM. Suspects there are now complete.	Ind.
28/7/15. BUSSEBOOM - BOESCHEPE Road.	Travelled slight Dressing station visited by D.M.S S.A. Cooper	Ind.
29/7/15. BUSSEBOOM - BOESCHEPE Road.	Inspected Dressing station, found that the manure heaps were being cleared from the farm. A good supply of lime has been obtained and a serious attempt is being made to deal with the fly problem. Large numbers of mosquitos are breeding in the pond "Culex".	
30/7/15. BUSSEBOOM - BOESCHEPE Road.	Visited A.D.M.S. and arranged certain matters in connection with the Dressing station. A.D.M.S.	Ind.

WAR DIARY

INTELLIGENCE SUMMARY.
(Erase heading not required.)

Army Form C. 2118.

Hour, Date, Place	Summary of Events and Information	Remarks and references to Appendices
30/7/15 (continued)	14th Division called to ask if I could arrange for him to visit aid posts, Dressing Station etc., in ever his Division will be taking over. Arranged to take him following day.	
31.7.15 BUSSEBOOM - BOESCHEPE Road.	A horse-show held today. 2 first prizes taken by teams from the 9th Field Ambulance - 1st open class (Heavy Draught), 1st class for Ambulance horses (Heavy Draught); 2nd third purple, 1st in single Heavy Draught class and 1 in 3 Ambulance Waggon turnouts complete. Visited in the morning advanced collecting post at CHATEAU ROSENTHAL and dressing stations accompanied by A.D.M.S. 3rd Division. End of July 1915. Diary relating to Dressing Station in OUDERDOM - DICKEBUSCH road by Capt. A.J. Trousdale R.A.M.C. is appended. G.W. Allen Lieut. Colonel, R.A.M.C O.C. No. 9 Field Ambulance	

Army Form C. 2118.

WAR DIARY
or
INTELLIGENCE SUMMARY.
(Erase heading not required.)

Instructions regarding War Diaries and Intelligence Summaries are contained in F.S. Regs., Part II. and the Staff Manual respectively. Title pages will be prepared in manuscript.

Hour, Date, Place	Summary of Events and Information	Remarks and references to Appendices
Farm by DICKEBUSCH		
6 p.m. 24-7-15 Wed.	Marches with B. Sect at 9 a.m to form Dressing Station. Arrived 12 noon. Capt. Fraser came with C. Sect. joining at 1.40 p.m. Lieut. Le Bas came with 24 Bearers. 2 hr/ Field Ambulance attached marches with me.	AWMcKuch Captain RAMC
10 A.M. 25-7-15.	Took over 6 wheeled stretcher carriers from No 8 F.A. McKuch proceeds Bearers No 4 Field Amb: under Lt Le Bas Captain to ROSENTHAL CHATEAU at 9.45 p.m. Collection of Wounded. 2 Motor Amb. Wagons proceeded to VOORMEZEELE under Lt NELLIE. 2 Motor Amb. Wagons proceeded to the BRASSERIE under Lt Martyn. Capt. Fraser RAMC proceeded with one car and Lt Douglas to ROSENTHAL CHATEAU at 12 mid night. 5 Wheeled stretcher carriers were left at ROSENTHAL CHATEAU with Bearers No 7 F.A. under Capt: Adams RAMC. Received orders to proceed to No 42 F.A. handed over to Captain Fraser RAMC	AWMcKuch captain RAMC

Army Form C. 2118.

WAR DIARY
or
INTELLIGENCE SUMMARY

(Erase heading not required.)

Instructions regarding War Diaries and Intelligence Summaries are contained in F.S. Regs., Part II. and the Staff Manual respectively. Title pages will be prepared in manuscript.

Hour, Date, Place	Summary of Events and Information	Remarks and references to Appendices
12 noon 25.7.15	Took over charge of drawing stores from Capt. Roberts. B. section are Engineers in Chg. on drawing stores. Attenuators - 22 wounded 19 sick. (1 officer)	Shaer. Capt. R.M.C.
12 noon 26.7.15	All available men are employed in clearing of the filth & arms heaps which were amongst me about the farm. These are to enormous as to constitute a real peat hush to avoid to when has the removed that at present there seems available there before any thing further is burned. The truck running to Furnes. DICKEBUSCH has been replaced by the foot Cav. as the trucks is more use to this line. R. Walter Hutchet is also added to the subsection time. Attenuators. Wounded 10. Sick 17.	P.

1247 W 3259 200,000 (E) 8/14 J.B.C. & A. Forms/C. 2118/11.

WAR DIARY or INTELLIGENCE SUMMARY

Army Form C. 2118.

Hour, Date, Place	Summary of Events and Information	Remarks and references to Appendices
12 noon 24.7.15	6 cars wanted to Scottish wood during forenoon to collect cases from wounded what were being sent up from VORMEZEELE. The ordinary routine for collection of cases is as follows:— 3 cars to ROSENTHAL CHATEAU. Leave at dusk. One car to remain behind there until 1 a.m, if not required for first trip, otherwise it will return & collect any cases which may come in during night. After previous return, i.e about 1.45 a.m, 3 cars proceed to BRASSERIE. One cases there return to dressing station & the remaining cars from there go to VORMEZEELE. If a car is then empty it proceeds to do the 1 am. trip, calling at all aid posts in VORMEZEELE & BRASSERIE. Admission — wounded 2 Officers, 5 o.men. Sick 19.	
12 noon 26.7.15	Changed with present through interpreter for several of James york canvas beds.	

Army Form C. 2118.

WAR DIARY
or
INTELLIGENCE SUMMARY
(Erase heading not required.)

Instructions regarding War Diaries and Intelligence Summaries are contained in F. S. Regs., Part II. and the Staff Manual respectively. Title pages will be prepared in manuscript.

Hour, Date, Place	Summary of Events and Information	Remarks and references to Appendices
28.7.15.	A.D.M.S. 5th Divn came with M.O. when evacuating men for C.C.S. Admissions – wounded 24. Sick – 3 Officers. 31 men.	A.P.
12 noon 29.7.15.	Wounded 26 O.R. 5th Divn had as a dressing station. Men has not been daily employed cleaning up sewage, emptying dustbins & refuse of farm, filling in holes in ground, &c. Admissions – 29 wounded, 18 sick (2 Officers).	A.P.
12 noon 30.7.15.	Yesterday 6 Abeele for lorry from Field Ambs. Douglas proceeded on a month's leave. Chateau with D.A.D.M.S. III Division. Admissions – 13 wounded, sick 25 (1 Officer).	A.P.
12 noon 31.7.15.	Much of farm yard manure has now been removed. Pits have been dried, & it is a day or 2 this Nothing ought to be sufficiently dried to have them carted thoroughly swept out & cleaned. Pass attachment.	

Army Form C. 2118.

WAR DIARY
or
INTELLIGENCE SUMMARY

(Erase heading not required.)

Instructions regarding War Diaries and Intelligence Summaries are contained in F. S. Regs, Part II. and the Staff Manual respectively. Title pages will be prepared in manuscript.

Hour, Date, Place	Summary of Events and Information	Remarks and references to Appendices
31.7./15	Z. Maken ROSENTHAL with A.D.M.S. III Division. + 6E, 9th M Amb., Lieut Wilson to ROULERS with A.D.M.S. 17th Division. Admissions - Wounded (1 Officer). 43 Sick (2 Officers)	[signatures]

www.ingramcontent.com/pod-product-compliance
Lightning Source LLC
Chambersburg PA
CBHW080922230426
43668CB00014B/2176